AN ANGEL AT MY SIDE

Joy,

Best Wishes And
Thank You For Your
Support!

Warm Regards,

Frances M Schindler
12/2/01

An Angel at My Side

Surviving Leukemia
Through Love

Frances M. Schindler

Writers Club Press
San Jose New York Lincoln Shanghai

An Angel at My Side
Surviving Leukemia Through Love

Writers Club Press
an imprint of iUniverse.com, Inc.

For information address:
iUniverse.com, Inc.
5220 S 16th, Ste. 200
Lincoln, NE 68512
www.iuniverse.com

To protect privacy, some names have been changed.

ISBN: 0-595-17599-6

Printed in the United States of America

Dedication

The Gift of Life

This book is dedicated to all the doctors, nurses, social workers, therapists and all the others who helped me get back on my feet again. And I offer an extra special "Thanks" to my loving sister, husband, family and friends.

Thank you for giving me back my life. You have made my life more meaningful than ever. I have learned through my experiences to be sincere, grateful, and helpful to others.

Contents

Introduction

Little did I know when a nurse once suggested I should start writing a journal, that it would become a published book.

I grew up in a small town in northern Wisconsin, where life was simple and undemanding. My happy-go-lucky father worked in the local hardware store until his death in the year 1984, and my loving mother dedicated her life to nurturing our family. I was the "baby of the family," with one older brother and an older sister who is also my best friend. We were a close-knit, middle-class Catholic family.

I left home in 1973 to attend technical school in Superior, Wisconsin, which was approximately one hundred miles from home. I shared an apartment with my sister and three other girls. The first year was one of the best times of my life. Freedom at last!

That would change the next year, when I naively decided to get married. After two and a half years of physical, emotional and controlling abuse, I divorced. The only good thing that came out of the marriage was a beautiful son.

I met a man who was climbing the corporate ladder. He had enormous energy from within, while I on the other hand was unstable and distraught from my divorce. Rick patiently and lovingly taught me to believe in myself and helped me regain my self-confidence. He literally swept me off my feet and took me places I had only dreamed about.

We moved to Milwaukee for a year, transferred to Minneapolis the second year, and finally settled in Illinois. Rick was also divorced and had two children, Nicole (Nikki) and Chris. Nikki and Chris lived with their mother in Upper Michigan and spent holidays and summers with us. My son, Brian, did not see his father after the divorce and has lived with us all his life, spending some summers with his grandmother.

Rick and I finally agreed to get married on July of 1983, after a three-year engagement. In April of 1986, our daughter, Allison, was born. We have been happily married now for seventeen years. We bought a small remitter's agent business in 1988, which I ran myself until my illness. My husband then decided to quit his job and take over the business. With his expertise, it is now one of the largest in northern Illinois.

In 1991, I was diagnosed with acute myelocytic leukemia. I immediately entered the hospital for three rounds of chemotherapy. After having had enough of hospitals, I decided against a bone marrow transplant, But in July of 1993, the leukemia came back and the bone marrow transplant took place. This book is an honest account of my seven-year battle with leukemia and severe graft versus host disease of the skin. I also experienced psychotic behavior due to a prescription drug. This is important, yet painful to tell.

I hope that by writing this book I can help others with similar experiences to know that they are not alone. Maybe my readers can learn from my mistakes.

A few years before I was diagnosed, I had been reading, with great interest, several books on spirituality, trying to find the true meaning of life. My own book does slant in that direction. I also had an enlightening encounter that needs to be told. You may not agree or believe in some of my out-of-the-way thinking, but that is okay. You have a right to your opinions and I have a right to mine. When you have death knocking at your door, the only thing that matters is what you truly believe in your heart and soul, despite all the ridicule around you. The only important aspect you care about is to SURVIVE.

Chapter 1

Shock and Denial

*It is amazing how a few words
can change your life forever.*

It was December 26, 1991, when I heard those dreadful words from my doctor. I couldn't believe my ears. "This can't be," I thought. "I'm only 36 years old." I felt that I had been issued a death sentence. I had children to raise, a business to run, and besides, it was the holiday season. This was bad timing. But, is there ever a good time to hear such news?

This all started when I wanted my husband, Rick, to have a physical examination, since he had not had one in years. He agreed, but only if I would have one, too. So, I made the appointments for just after Thanksgiving.

The doctor ran many tests on both of us. When the results came back, my husband's tests proved to be normal. However, my blood count was a little lower than usual, and the doctor wanted me to come back the following week for another blood test.

I didn't think too much about this at the time and brushed it aside. I had been feeling a little more tired than usual, but it was the holiday season and I was running around after work shopping for Christmas presents. I think back now and realize that my body was trying to tell me something, but I was afraid to listen.

The following week, I went to the lab and another blood sample was drawn. This time, the blood count was even lower than the first test. The doctor sat me down in his office and told me that this could mean I was anemic. It could also be the first sign of leukemia. He stated that it was too early to draw any conclusions, but he did want to be honest with me and let me know of the possibility of leukemia. I was to come back in one week for a repeat blood test, and he would then decide what steps should be taken. I walked out of his office stunned. This could not possibly be true. I locked the thought away in my subconscious mind.

During the next week a very strange encounter happened to me. A frequent customer visited my office and told me that his son had just been diagnosed with leukemia. Reluctantly, I asked him what his son's symptoms were. The man explained that there were no symptoms, but that he had passed out for no apparent reason. He was taken to the hospital, where tests were run. When his test results came back, they showed he had a very low blood count.

I felt my heart racing. My stomach started to burn and I felt nauseous. This was exactly what my doctor had told me. I tried to keep my composure until the customer left. I had been reading about the phenomenon of synchronicity by the Swiss psychologist Carl Jung. Synchronicity is the perception of meaningful coincidences that move human beings toward a greater growth in consciousness. I instantly went into the back room and began to shake. I tried to convince myself that this was just a strange, unrelated coincidence.

Since I had confided in my friend, Karen, about the tests, I immediately called her and told her what had just happened. She calmed me down and told me not to jump to any conclusions. She told me to clarify the situation and go ahead and get another blood test and talk to my doctor. I hung up the phone and took some deep breaths. Before I called the doctor, I realized that I may have asked for this. In the last couple of years, I had been reading a lot about how we manifest our own illnesses. Could this actually be true? I shook my head and instantly put the idea out of my mind.

After work that night, I stopped and bought myself a well-known and respected medical book. I checked the page explaining the CBC test. The initials "CBC" actually stand for a Complete Blood Count. The term "count" refers to the counting of each type of blood cell in a given volume of blood. It also measures the percentage of red blood cells, the number and kinds of white blood cells, and the number of platelets. The red cells' function is to give out enough oxygen for us to survive. The platelets help the blood to clot. The white blood cells defend the body against foreign matter such as infections.

I hesitantly looked up *leukemia* for the definition and accompanying symptoms. Easy bruising, tiredness, night sweats, fever, and infections were some of the symptoms. I checked my body and didn't see any bruises. I took my temperature and it was 99.5 degrees, which I didn't think much of at the time. I decided to have another blood test taken the next day, just before Rick and I went out of town for the weekend to celebrate Christmas with his family. We left as soon as I got back from the lab. I really didn't want to know what the results were until we returned, because I didn't want to spoil our mini-vacation.

Rick's parents organize the Christmas weekend in a hotel within their town and reserve a room for each family at poolside. The children really have fun enjoying the pool and being with all their cousins. On Saturday night, we all sat around, opened presents, and celebrated Christmas.

After the celebration, I started to feel clammy. This is the only way I can describe the way I felt within. I confided in Rick, and he assured me that everything would be okay, no matter what happened. We decided not to discuss it with other family members until we knew for sure what it was. I felt that something was terribly wrong with me.

We arrived home late on Sunday night. As I put on my pajamas, I noticed some black and blue marks on my body. I was so exhausted I just crawled into bed and tried to sleep. That night, I awoke to find my whole body soaked with perspiration. The night sweats had begun.

First thing Monday morning, my doctor called me at the office. He said he had been trying to reach me all weekend. It seemed my blood count was dangerously low and that he wanted to set up an appointment with a specialist that afternoon. He explained that they would be doing a lot of blood work and a procedure called a bone marrow biopsy.

This was making me very nervous. He gave me the name of the doctor I would be seeing, and I was trying hard to concentrate on what he was telling me. In a daze, I hung up the phone. I immediately called Rick at work and discussed what the doctor had told me. Rick said he would pick me up and take me to the clinic, and for me to try not to worry about it. I hung up the phone and discussed the situation with my assistant. We convinced each other that it couldn't be leukemia. I was probably just anemic. I attempted not to worry about it, and made an effort to enjoy an office Christmas party while waiting for Rick.

We entered the medical building and looked at the directory. I had misplaced the doctor's name and could only remember that his last name started with an "E." I found a last name beginning with that letter on the directory.

We took the elevator up and walked into the office. Some of the women in the waiting area seemed to be pregnant. The receptionist handed me a form to fill out, and as I started filling out the form I realized that the questions all related to being pregnant, which I knew I was not. Rick insisted that we were in the wrong office. As I returned the form to the receptionist, she handed me a specimen cup. Puzzled, I asked the receptionist why she needed a urine sample when my blood was the problem.

Now she was the one that looked puzzled. She informed me that I was in the wrong office and needed to see the hematologist/oncologist on the first floor. (At the time, I didn't even know what these two words meant.) His last name also began with the same letter and both names did sound alike. I humbly walked out with my husband.

We finally got to the right office, late, and I was emotionally stressed out. We checked in and sat down. I noticed that some of the people in the waiting room were bald and looked deathly ill. I also noticed a lot of pamphlets on the wall….skin cancer, breast cancer, lymphoma, LEUKEMIA. The word jumped out at me and I took a deep breath. I began to realize what "hematology" and "oncology" mean. One is the study of blood and the other is the study of cancer. I knew I was in trouble.

After what seemed like an eternity, my name was finally called. The nurse first had me go to the lab to get my blood drawn. They did all kinds of blood work, sticking my arms with so many needles, so many times that I thought my arm would fall off.

Rick and I were then put into an examination room. The doctor walked in, and my first impression was that he looked much younger than myself. He asked me many personal questions and did a routine physical exam. I was afraid to ask him any questions, fearing what he might say to me. He told us that the blood tests would have to come back before they could make any kind of diagnosis. I needed to come back for a bone marrow biopsy first thing tomorrow. Then they would know more. Tomorrow was to be Christmas Eve.

We drove home in silence. My mind felt like it was going to explode. I didn't want to think what the problem might be. At times like this it's almost like you already know what is happening, but your subconscious won't tell your conscious mind.

Our four kids—my son Brian, our daughter Allison, and my two step-children, Nikki and Chris—were waiting for us at home. Thank goodness the three older kids were in their teens and basically took care of themselves. But we had a little five-year-old who did not understand what was happening except what she heard from her siblings. I could only imagine what was going through her mind. We informed Nikki, who was waiting at the door when we got home, and the others, that we did not know what it was yet and we had to go back the next day and do more tests. I had a very hard time sleeping that night.

The next day, Rick and I were at the doctor's office first thing in the morning. They did more blood tests. My arms were throbbing with pain. After we had spent half of a day there, they decided not to do the bone marrow biopsy until after Christmas. The explanation they gave was that the lab would not be open on Christmas Day. They would definitely do it the day after Christmas and then would be able to tell me exactly what was going on. Personally, I think they just didn't want to tell me the day before Christmas and ruin the holiday for me.

So, Christmas Day came. I watched my children opening their presents and thought it just might be my last. I shuddered at the thought. We had a lot of company that day, so I kept myself busy. Both sides of our family called and wished us a Merry Christmas. We decided not to mention the doctor's visits. I couldn't help but think of that bone marrow biopsy tomorrow. They told me it would be very painful, but that it would only last a few seconds. I hate pain. I'm a big baby. I just wanted to get it over with. Sleeping that night was hopeless.

Finally, morning arrived and we drove to the doctor's office. They did the biopsy. I tried not to look at any of the instruments they used. They apparently stick a needle into the back of the pelvic bone, sucking up bone marrow into a syringe. You get to choose what side you want them to take it from. It is very painful, but is over in seconds.

Now we just had to wait for the lab to give us the results. I took a break and stepped out of the office. Another patient was having a cigarette in the hall. I saw the doctor walk out through his back door and walked into the lab. The patient and I started to talk. He told me that the doctor had told him he only had a few months to live and that he was making plans to spend his last days with his family. He had lung cancer and seemed to accept it. I couldn't believe how at ease he seemed to be. I was shocked at his attitude. This was something I couldn't handle at that time.

Rick saw the expression on my face and made up something so that we could go back into the office and sit down. That was not what I needed to hear right then. Everything was happening so fast that I did not have time to focus. I was really getting scared. What if they gave me a death sentence? What would I do? The waiting became agony.

Finally, they called us into a room. My husband squeezed my hand tight as we walked down the hall. The doctor sat us back in his room and told us the bad news. It looked as though I had acute myelocytic leukemia. I only heard the last word. My husband and I looked at each other, horrified. My mind began to wander, and I thought of the only two people I knew who had had it–and they had died after only a few months. I was in total shock.

My doctor informed me I had to go into the hospital and start treatments as soon as possible. I just couldn't believe this. He called the nurse to do a chest x-ray. She brought me into the x-ray room and I lost it. I couldn't help it. I started to cry hysterically and couldn't stop. The nurse gave me a big hug and comforted me. I took a few big breaths and regained control of myself. I finally managed to get through the x-ray. We walked back and met my husband in the doctor's room. We were given instructions and advice on how to handle the situation ourselves and with family and friends. My husband also wanted to get a second opinion. The doctor agreed with him, and we chose to go to University Hospital in Madison, Wisconsin. Our doctor called and set up an appointment for the next day. He had given us the entire lab and blood tests to take with us to have them analyzed. He wished us good luck.

There was silence in the car all the way home. I decided to put up a brick wall inside my mind and throw all my emotions behind it. I had to be brave for the kids and fight like hell for my life. There was no time to feel sorry for myself. I could do that after it was all done. But right then I had to stay focused, using tunnel vision, so to speak.

I believe we all follow a path that we ourselves have set, and that we have spiritual guides to lead the way. I had a funny feeling that this was mine. I had to make a decision to get through this and to believe that this was happening to me for a reason, which was to send my life in the right direction. So I guess this was my so-called test of life. I would just have to take it and pass.

The kids would have to learn to live without me for awhile until I got better. I would have to place all my energy into beating this thing. My husband would have all the responsibility for the family. I would have to focus on myself. I knew it was going to be very hard for him, both physically and emotionally. But also, I knew he could handle it. He is a very strong and determined man—but working a full-time job and coming home to another full-time job is not easy.

I think that was something us baby boomers didn't think about when we wanted to go to work. It was great that both parents worked and had that second income, but what we really forgot was who was going to mind the store. When we were young, most of us had a stay-at-home mom who took care of all the domestic responsibilities, while our fathers worked to support the family. Mom met all of the kid's needs. Now, we had to train ourselves in that both mother and father had to take on equal obligations for our children. But having a sick wife on top of it would prove to be very hard.

I decided not to walk in crying in front of the children, but to be brave. My husband sat all the kids down and broke the news to them. Brian broke down, put his arms around me and began to cry. My two stepchildren joined in, with our 5-year-old watching and taking it all in. I told them not to worry about me, and that "I am tough and I will conquer this disease." I had no idea what to say to my little one. As I put Allison to bed that night, I tried to explain to her what was happening to me and that I might have to go into the hospital. I hoped that she understood some of what I told her. I couldn't bear the thought of her growing up without a mother. I also worried about Brian. Since Rick had never legally adopted him, I was not sure what would happen to him.

The next day, we drove into Madison to get our second opinion. They confirmed the diagnosis. They discussed a bone marrow transplant after my treatments, which could be handled there, but in the meantime I was to have the treatments close to home.

On the way home, I informed my husband that if anything happened to me I wanted to be cremated. He could have a wake, but I didn't want to be buried six feet under. I don't know why I had to say that at that time. I thought I might not have a chance to talk about it again. Besides, if something did happen, my family wouldn't have to worry about as many details while mourning my death.

As soon as we arrived home, I contacted my doctor and discussed my protocol. I was to enter the hospital the next morning to begin my first round of chemotherapy.

One of the hardest tasks was phoning my side of the family. They all live in another state. Rick started the process. He called my sister, who is also my best friend, and broke the news to her. The doctor had given me some good advice. He told me to call the relatives and only talk a few minutes and then hang up. I was advised to then wait for awhile to let the initial shock sink in, and to call again.

When I called her back, we talked for a long time. To get through this, we decided that we both would be brave, no matter what happened. She's my big sister and has always been there for me. She's the kind of sister that would do anything for me. I can call her anytime, and she is always there to listen. I have only one other sibling, an older brother. I tried to call him, but he was not home. I left a message on his machine to call me.

The agonizing call was yet to come. I have no doubt that when my mother dies, she will become a saint in heaven. She is the most loving and caring human being I know. She has dedicated her whole life to her family and is always there for us, never asking for anything in return. She is a sincere woman with simple needs, always looking at the positive things in life. My father was also a wonderful, kind, caring person who enjoyed just a simple life. (Actually, when I was growing up, I thought it *too* simple and boring.) We had a *Leave It to Beaver* life in a *Mayberry* type of town, located in Northern Wisconsin. It took us a long time to get over our father's death sixteen years ago, and now I had to phone mom and inform her of this news.

I inhaled a deep breath and dialed the number. I started out making small talk and ultimately related the news. There was dead silence on the other end. I heard a heavy sigh and immediately recognized anguish in her voice. I told her not to worry and that I would get through this. We hung up and I called her back a few minutes later. I asked her to come down and help take care of the family. This would be the best way for her to cope with the situation. She agreed and made arrangements to take the bus down, since she doesn't know how to drive. Rick also conversed with his side of the family.

Since I would be going into the hospital the next day and would be there for quite awhile, I needed to get my business affairs in order. I gave full reins to my devoted assistant to run my business until I get back. We also called a friend of ours to help out while I was away, since Rick had no knowledge or experience in running the business. I then spent some quality time with my family. I had my little daughter help me pack so I could get her prepared. I also packed a few enlightening books that I had been reading lately. They had helped me get through some tough times before, and I sure needed them now. That night, I opened up the Bible and began to read the New Testament.

drug was in a bag on the IV pole and infused through the tubes attached to the bag and the chest. The chemo started, and was to continue 24 hours a day for seven days.

At this point I was not sure if this IV pole I would have to carry around everyday was a friend or an enemy. This mechanism was a long pole with a machine attached to it with tubes coming out of it. These tubes got connected to the tubes that had been inserted during surgery. The IV pole was on wheels and had to be taken with me wherever I went. The pole and the tubes were like an obstacle course, especially when going to the bathroom at night. I always seemed to get tangled up in the cord somehow. I decided that since it was going to be with me for awhile, I might as well give it a name. From that point on I referred to my IV pole as "*Fred*." Fred ran on battery power, so you did not have to have him plugged in all the time. He did, however, become a nuisance when he did not work right. He got very frustrated and made a loud beeping sound. It really got on my nerves. I would have to call a nurse to fix him. He's a very sensitive kind of guy. My chest was really sore the next day from the surgery, but I learned to live with it. It made me uneasy to see the tubes loosely hanging from me. I decide to start wearing a bra all the time and stuff them inside.

Now, these hospital routines started very early in the morning. The lab girl would come by everyday at 5:30 a.m. to take blood from my tubes. She would walk in, turn on the lights, and greet me with a cheery hello. It was very annoying. Another nurse would come in next and take my vital signs and bring me a tray full of pills to take. (I was a person who very rarely even took an aspirin.) This pill taking was not a good sign.

A few minutes later a breakfast tray would arrive. My room was Grand Central Station. After breakfast, the staff encouraged me to take a shower. Taking a shower is no easy task, since you have tubes sticking out of you. The Groshong catheter would have to be taped with plastic by the nurse so it wouldn't get wet. Fred would stand right outside the shower door and would have to wait for me. (He doesn't like getting wet.) Going to the bathroom was also a humiliating experience. The nurse would put a container in the toilet to catch everything. It was degrading, especially when the doctor or friends would stop in for a visit and the nurse hadn't cleaned the container yet. I learned to keep the bathroom door closed.

The doctor would come in the room every morning to check on me. I saw the doctor more than I saw my own family. I felt so dependent on this person who was trying to save my life. I have a great admiration for this man. An infectious disease doctor also paid a visit every day. I received many flowers, plants, cards, and phone calls from all my family and friends. Everyone was supportive and wonderful. They were all concerned, but hesitant as what to say. I felt like I was to be associated as a whole different person from now on. I even received some beautiful meditating music tapes from a girl who works with my sister, whom I had never met. They were soothing to listen to. My books were always at my bedside, even though I couldn't seem to read. The nurses informed me that the flowers and plants I received would have to go after the chemo treatments, since they might be carrying something that could make my immune system weaker.

Sitting in my hospital bed, I started to think of the first time I questioned my life on this earth. I think we all go through this at one point in our lives and ask the big question, *"What's it all about?"* It was about five years ago for me. I was at the mall by myself and went past a bookstore. A book on display caught my eye about a person searching to find the true meaning of life. It talked about how important it was to love ourselves first before we can love others and how each and every one of us has a purpose in this life. Today I still do not know why I was so compelled to buy this book. The strange thing about it is that I didn't like to read books, nor did I have the time. I almost felt like I was in a trance buying this book. As soon as I got home, I began to read it. It started to change my whole way of thinking. The book made me take a good hard look at my life and how to change it in a positive way.

Positive things started to happen to me. Just as I was finishing the book, the movie about the book came out. It was all so incredible to me. I started to read more about karma (What you put out into the world, you get back in return), the power of positive thinking and how each and everyone of us has a purpose in this life and how we need to find that purpose and soar with it. I tried to analyze it and compare it to the teachings in the Bible. I read and reread the Bible, especially the messages and parables Jesus had said during his existence on this planet. They are such simple phrases. *"Ask, and it shall be given. Seek, and you shall find."* Don't get me wrong, I am not trying to preach to anyone. I am just trying to find the true meaning of life for myself.

Around this time, I was offered the opportunity to buy a business from a friend who wanted to sell. I convinced my husband I could do it, and I really believed in myself. I felt that I was on a huge "HIGH" without drugs. If you had told me a few years ago that I would own my own business, I would have told you that you were crazy. But I did take over this business, and it is still very successful today.

I also investigated and bought a tape on visualization to explore this strange phenomenon. Visualization is a technique to reach out to your spiritual guides. It is also a form of meditation. (I know, I know, you are going to think I have really lost it now, but there are also spiritual guides in the Bible.) I went home and played the tape. You start out visualizing a vase. A vase immediately came to mind–the color, shape, and texture. I immediately visualized that it was sitting on a stone near an old water well, maybe in the Middle East somewhere. I figured it was just my imagination, so I went along with it. But in my imagination, I actually didn't see anyone. Then I gave up. I can't do this, I thought. I couldn't concentrate. Maybe I was trying too hard or just couldn't accept it. This seemed just all too silly and frustrating, but I always found myself going back to the bookstore reading more and more on Eastern philosophy,

Edgar Casey, Nostradamus, and many other spiritual books. I was also surprised that many famous historians and scientists also believed in this way of thinking. For some reason gave me strength in everything I did. Whenever I would go away from it, which was a lot of times, my life became unbalanced.

Sometimes I couldn't handle what was being said and had to stop reading, not being able to go back to it for almost a year. I think that may be due to my strict Catholic upbringing. Somehow I was trying desperately to find a happy medium (no pun intended) between the two. I even blocked the whole concept out of my mind for a while. But I always found myself going back to it. It was fulfilling, but yet at the same time confusing and so bizarre. Maybe I just wasn't ready to be true to myself or accept this out-of-this-world way of thinking. In the past couple of years, I had started to feel that I was on a roller coaster ride.

The room I was in was of average size. I always dressed every day in my own clothes, never wearing hospital gowns. I also put my makeup on everyday and styled my hair. I decided to do some exercises and yoga every day in the hospital, as long as I felt okay. When I think about it, this really wasn't so bad. I couldn't remember the last time I could just lounge around all day. I was used to going a hundred miles an hour, working full time at my business and coming home to another full-time job. This would be a mini-vacation for me. I typically never had the time to watch TV, especially in the afternoon. It was a new experience for me. Everyday, I walked around the halls and tried to find someone to strike up a conversation with. I'd call my office everyday and obtain the agenda from my assistant and talk over any problems. I don't know what I would have done without her. I know this was a lot for her. She had to put her education on hold and never once asked for anything in return. I will always appreciate what she has done for me.

I would try everyday to look as normal as possible. I telephoned my family and friends often to be in contact with the outside world. When I got depressed, I would always call my closest friend from high school.

Mary could make me laugh and always brightened my day. She always had a joke. She's one of those people who can always be the life of a dull party. She has a great gift for life.

I looked outside my window and it was another gloomy day. I tried to take a negative and turn it into a positive. I guess if you have to go into the hospital, this is the best time to do it. It is the most boring month of the year. I am surprised how normal I still felt, having chemotherapy drugs filling my veins in the past couple of days. I knew this chemo would destroy my immune system, the bad cells and the good ones. Research hasn't come up with any solutions to correct that problem yet. But I know they are working on it. I drank at least a pitcher of water every day and visualized the chemo flowing out of my body and not staying too long in one place.

Rick's parents came down for the weekend. They were very support- ive. They left Sunday and took my two step-kids home to Michigan. Rick and my other two kids, Brian and Ally, came for a visit Sunday night. I could see the stress and strain this had been for my husband. I felt so sorry for him. Life was so good to us until now. I guess we all have some bumpy roads to get through in our lives, and we just have to deal with them as best as we know how.

My mother was to be here Monday night on the bus, to stay and help out until I could come home. Our best friends, Mary and Ray, came down to visit from Milwaukee. They brought me a shaggy stuffed dog. He was soft and fluffy. That night, the lady who was supposed to have been my roommate across the hall died. Relatives were in her room mourning her death. I grabbed the stuffed animal and silently cried myself to sleep. It gave me so much comfort to hold unto something that I slept with it every night. I didn't care what anyone thought. I decide to name it "Therapy" because that's what it gave me on those lonely hospital nights.

Well, it had been a week and I finally got off the IV machine. As soon as they unhooked me I skipped through the halls...."I'm free!" This was so great! I was so excited. I knew it would be just a little thing, but it felt like I had been let out of prison.

That night, my family came to see me. My mom brought me some home cooking, since I couldn't seem to stomach the hospital food. Perhaps the chemo had something to do with my lack of appetite. My husband stopped by every morning before work and brought me breakfast. It seemed like the family was doing okay without me. My sister and her family were expected the next day. While she was here, she was to be tested by my doctor to see if she was a match for a bone marrow transplant. I couldn't wait to see her. That night, however, I started to feel irritable. By the next morning I had a sore throat, fever and chills. By the afternoon I was feeling pretty lousy. My sister and her husband walked in.

It was good to see them, but my enthusiasm was fading. I felt so weak that I just wanted to sleep. Rick came in and brought me supper. I was so tired that I couldn't eat a bite. I ended up falling asleep in front of everyone.

The next couple of days I spent sleeping. I didn't feel much like having company, and everyone stayed away. My sister and family came to say goodbye. I could hardly talk, and I felt so awful that I started to cry. I didn't get a chance to visit very much and spend precious time with her. She tried to comfort me before she left. It was so hard to say goodbye. I felt like it might be my last time.

Over the next two days I became very ill. I could hardly get out of bed just to go to the bathroom. It was like having the worst flu, but ten times greater. Your only hope is to feel slightly better the next day.

On the fifteenth day in the hospital, I was infused with blood and platelets. Within a few hours, I began to feel much better. I had a really good day. It felt good to be alive. My strength seemed to be coming back. I cleaned my room with my headphones on, listening to the radio for the first time since I'd been there. It felt good to be back in the real world.

At first I had lots of company, but has really slowed down. I would watch the clock until the family would be there. Sometimes they couldn't visit, and then it would be a long day and a lonely night. One thing I had done was to start a journal. A nurse had suggested it to pass the time away. It turned out to be a great idea.

It was now the eighteenth day and I was beginning to feel the walls closing in. I had to have an IV in me four times a day for about two hours each. I couldn't even move around, which was getting on my nerves. I went to take a shower and clumps of hair fell out. I had the nurse come in and cut the rest off. Losing my hair was not such a big deal to me. A perm put in my hair a few months ago had turned out dry, split, and damaged, so starting over wasn't so bad.

I had forgotten to get a wig. My girlfriend, Debbie, brought me a turban and some fake bangs to place under the turban so it looked like I had hair. She and I had fun playing around with it. I played around with this turban for a couple of days. It just seemed so flat on my head that I thought of an idea. I took maxi pads, tore off the sticky strips and put the pads on the inside roof of the turban. It kept my head warm and was soft on my scalp, giving me height at the same time. I was always willing to try anything new.

On the twenty-first day in the hospital I had my first opportunity to leave the floor, on the condition that I wear a mask. Rick, Allison and I went to the hospital cafeteria to get something to eat. It felt so good to get away from my room. My mom, Brian and his girlfriend came up to join us and we had a nice visit.

At night, I usually had a lengthy conversation with God. I talked to him as if he were my own dad. I asked him to help and guide me through this, and also to help me make sense of all this new way of thinking I had been reading about. When you have death knocking at your door, you do a lot of analyzing of your life. I thought about my life and asked myself if I had done anything in this world to make a difference. The only thing I could think of was that I had bore two children. I wasn't a bad person, but I just hadn't done anything to help mankind. To explore my own spiritual quest seemed to be a new positive beginning for me. Maybe this disease was to be the end of an old life and a fresh beginning of a new life. I closed my eyes and tried to meditate on the chakra system I had read about. The chakra system consists of seven energy fields of color that are aligned within us from head to toe. This technique originated thousands of years ago in the East to get in touch with spirituality. As one meditates on each color and location on the body he or she concentrates as it gets brighter and brighter and spins within the person. One visualizes it cleansing or healing that part of the body. The first chakra is the color red and is based at the root of the spine. This chakra involves our physical dimension understanding. The second chakra is the color orange and is located in the sexual organs and deals with our relationships and sexuality. The third chakra is the color yellow and sits in the middle of the stomach. This is where the intuition or "Gut" feeling is. The fourth chakra is the color green, the heart chakra, yielding the power of love. The fifth chakra is the color blue and is at the throat. This chakra gives us our power, spirituality, and communication. The sixth chakra is the color indigo and is located at the forehead. This particular chakra goes beyond our physical dimension. (I am not quite sure what that means; I am still struggling with this one.) It brings out our higher self, and it can be used to make our lives better. The seventh and final chakra is the combination of violet and white light. It is located on top of the head. I envisioned each and every one of these and meditated on each one to rid the leukemia cells within me. I remembered reading about a little boy who had a hole in his heart and concentrated on a needle and thread sewing him back up. When the doctors took another x-ray, the hole was no longer there.

Chapter 3

Homeward Bound

Laughter can be the best medicine.

Great news! My counts were up! If they would stay that way by the next day, I would get to go home. Some more great news! My sister seemed to be a close match for me on the bone marrow. I don't know why, but we both had talked about it and we were pretty sure that our instincts knew we were a match. I now had a second defense. They were to do another bone marrow biopsy on me that morning, and then I would get to go home by noon. I was in such a great mood. Everything was running smoothly. I skipped around the halls and visited the cafe. I could not wait to get out of here. I spent most of the day out of my room and talking on the phone. I was sure glad to have a calling card. I needed to get a wig once I got out of here. I was tired of wearing a turban.

Finally, the next day arrived. I waited impatiently for the doctor to perform another bone marrow biopsy. It was done right in the room. The nurse came in and revealed my blood count. Doctor said I could go home by noon. I telephoned Rick to make arrangements for him to pick me up. Anxiously, I waited for the hospital release papers to be drawn up. I had been in this place for twenty-four days. Finally, I endorsed the papers, just as Rick entered the room. He grabbed my suitcase and off we went. The attendant wheeled me down to the front door where Rick was waiting with the car. It sure was strange getting into a car. I always looked at them from my hospital window and wondered where everyone was going. Now I was getting to go somewhere. What a great feeling! I just couldn't wait to sleep in my own bed. My home felt like a castle—there were so many rooms to go to. I had so much missed my home.

It was so good to see my mom. My husband was so excited to have me home; I could see it in his warm eyes. My children came home from school and we exchanged many hugs. I didn't want to let them go. We all had a wonderful night. I couldn't wait to go to bed and sleep right beside the man I love.

My next appointment to see my doctor wasn't for four days. You would think I would be happy about this, but up until then I hadn't gone that long without him. I almost felt abandoned, and it made me somewhat nervous. I also had a problem sleeping at night. I would sleep most of the day and be up most of the night. I felt like an infant who had gotten her days and nights mixed up. But the worst problem was always feeling tired and weak. You just can't get enough rest. I wasn't really much help around the house. Thank goodness my mother was still there to help out. I don't know what we would have done without her. I also had to learn to change the dressing on my catheter every day to prevent infection.

On January 27, I finally went back to the doctor's office. The bone marrow biopsy taken in the hospital was still showing 10-20% bad cells. I would need another chemo treatment when my counts came up. They were to do another biopsy the next day. They finally give me a drug to relax me instead of doing the biopsy cold turkey, and I wondered why they hadn't given it to me before. They also checked my blood count. I spent another exhausting day at the doctor's office. I went to bed as soon as we got home. I phoned the doctor the next morning and found out that my counts were already up. I would be back in the hospital for another round of chemo starting tomorrow. I'd only been home a week and already would have to go back in. I was disappointed and hoped it wouldn't take too long.

So, the next morning I said good-bye to my family and checked in again. They hooked me up to "Fred" right away. I was not too happy to see him. I hoped that he would behave himself this time. By the next day, I had become very irritated. I couldn't seem to sit still. My period was back. I called the nurse in and told her how I was feeling. I needed something to calm me down. I felt like I was going to explode. I don't know what she gave me, but it sure did the trick. You really have to ask for things when you think you need them. This was very hard for me to do for awhile. I always wanted to do things for myself and not have to depend on anyone or anything for any help, but I realized that I did not have to suffer needlessly. All you have to do is make your ego get out of the way.

The next day I was allowed to go outside for awhile. It felt good to get some fresh air and to be out of the hospital bed. There were chairs to sit on outside and many patients were there with their IV poles. Fred was always by my side.

My assistant manager came in to visit that night. She brought a very funny booklet with her for me to read. As I started to read it, I couldn't seem to see the words too well. They just looked cloudy to me. She had to read the rest to me. (I guess this happens to some people temporarily who have chemo and it clears up later.) I hadn't laughed so hard in such a long while, and I laughed until my sides hurt. I guess laughter is the best medicine.

On the sixth day I got off the chemo machine and I also got to go home. My counts were still good (platelets 46,000 and WIC 1.2). But I had to be very careful, because the counts would be dropping during the next few days and I would have to stay in really close contact with the doctor's office. I would have to take my temperature four times a day, and if it was above 100.5 degrees I would immediately have to call the doctor. I would be taking floxin 1 per day, allopurinol 2 times daily and compazine if nausea set in. I would have to stay away from anyone who was sick and stay inside. I waited impatiently for that last drop of chemo to go through my veins so I could get out of here. My husband was out of town, so my girlfriend Debbie took time off of work to pick me up. I still had to go through the red tape of the hospital procedures. My discharge papers were finally done.

We got home and my mother had just made a homemade apple pie. (mmmm) It was heaven! Rick came home and he was surprised and happy that I was home again. My daughter seemed to be quiet and shy, but glad to see me. It was nice to be home again and eat regular food. I hated the hospital food. It made me nauseous. I still had a hard time sleeping at night. Running to the bathroom constantly was a regular routine. (It became my second home.) I also was very, very weak. The next day I went in as an outpatient to get two pints of blood and platelets. The platelets were cold going in. I could feel it all over my body. Sometimes my temperature fluctuated when I was receiving my infusions, but that was about it. When they first infused me with blood, I was worried about the AIDS scare that was going on and also afraid of getting a bad reaction from it. Once it's in you, you can't take it out. But that fear went away in time. The worst is to just sit there and wait until the infusion was done. It took a couple of hours. The next day I felt so much better; it was an energy boost.

The next day, I went back into the doctor's office. My counts were all normal. I got to take two weeks off and go back to a normal routine. I asked my doctor if I could go out to a dinner, and he gave his consent. My husband had told me that our friends had invited us to a dinner dance at a local country club and that if I was up to it we could go. I certainly was. I couldn't wait to get all dressed up, see my friends and be myself again. I picked out my black skirt and red blouse with my black and red high heels to match. I wore my *evening-wear* wig. It was very important to me to look as elegant as I could possibly look. As we got to the country club, I realized that it was Valentine's Day. The place was exquisitely decorated with this theme. It was so good to get out and be with people. I remember sitting beside my husband and talking to a friend. The band started to play the song, "*Lady in Red.*" I felt a gentle hand grasping mind and a whispered voice in my ear asking me to dance. Rick waltzed me out unto the dance floor. We joined hands and he swept me off my feet as we romantically waltzed, looking into each other's eyes. He is such a great dancer. I felt like we were the only ones out there. It was a very romantic, unforgettable night.

I didn't have to go back to the doctor's office for awhile. But after a few days of freedom, I started to panic. I was afraid of everything, because you don't want to get an infection or get sick again. I took my daughter to McDonald's, and as I entered the building I pulled my sleeves over my hands to touch the doorknob. I washed my hands constantly, afraid of picking up something. Every ache and pain I had, I panicked, worrying that it was back. I was very careful about the friends my children brought home, making sure they or others in their families were not sick. I noticed when I read the paper that I couldn't help but to check out the obituaries. Only time eases these emotions.

My mother had been at my house for over a month now, and I knew she really wanted to go home. It had been long and hard time for her. I really appreciated everything she had done for us. We wanted to make arrangements to bring her home, but as usual she wouldn't think of it and just wanted to take the bus home. I finally agreed with her wishes.

In the next two weeks, I tried to make my life as normal as possible. I just tried to pick up where I had left off. I still had energy. The second chemo didn't give me any ill effects. I'd been doing so well, my spirits were up and I still had my positive attitude. I went back to the doctor's office at the end of the second week. We did another bone marrow biopsy. I was displeased in what he told me: I would have to go into the hospital for a five-day treatment. I was having a drug called ARA-c 300ccs for three hours every 12 hours and having lederle 3 times during the week. Nausea on this one set in. This was the first time I had gotten sick. Normally I had been given the drug zolfran to help stop the nausea before the chemo treatments and it worked well. But not this time. All I did was sleep and try not to move too much. I was miserable all week.

I got to go home on the fifth day. Rick came to pick me up. I still didn't feel well. I stayed in bed at home for two straight days. I was feeling nauseous, had stomach pains, and was all around just miserable. My mouth was really starting to hurt and I could hardly eat. The tubes inside me hurt. The next day I spent five hours in the hospital for blood and platelets. I thought that would make me feel better. It didn't. My temperature was up and down. By March 25th, I was back in the hospital. I was feeling worse. My tubes were really hurting now. A biopsy was taken by where the tubes were and an infection was discovered. The tubes would have to come out. Some other doctor came into my room and tried to pull them out. The pain was excruciating. The tubes were attached to my skin. I would have punched the guy if I had had the strength.

I also had been in agony with my mouth. Painkillers didn't help. It felt as if someone had shot me in the mouth point blank and just left me there to suffer. My husband came into my room and I told him that I couldn't take it anymore. Up to then I had hardly complained to him, but this was unbearable. I know he felt helpless, knowing he couldn't do anything but watch me suffer. It must have been an awful feeling for him.

That afternoon, I was finally taken down to surgery to get the tubes out. In a couple of days I felt better. But now they would have to stick me with needles when they wanted to draw blood. Sometimes it took a couple of pokes before they would actually see blood. Several nurses tried to put an IV in my hand. After several attempts, it was finally in. It was a very painful experience. I was suffering all day.

Little did I know the worst was yet to come. I awakened in the middle of the night freezing so badly that my teeth were chattering. The nurse came in and covered me with more blankets. Then all of a sudden, I spiked a 104 temperature and I felt like I was on fire. This happened several times that night, first freezing and then hot. Somehow the nurse and I made it through it. She did a very good job. I found out that this happens to other patients. They also have a name for it: "*shake and bake.*"

The next day I received a call from my son. He had moved in with a friend. The tension between him and Rick had been too great for him to stay at home. It seemed that my family was falling apart. It had been very stressful for all of them. I didn't know if I had enough strength to handle this news. My sister called and I disclosed the problem. She decided to come down with her family over the weekend and help with the situation. I hung up feeling relieved. I just wanted so much for my family to get along. Brian's real father had never been in his life since we divorced when he was two. Rick was the only father that Brian had ever known. Rick is a strict disciplinarian, and dealing with a sixteen-year-old had to be tough. I know it was also hard on Brian, not knowing what would happen to him if something were to happen to me. I was sure that my situation was taking a toll on both of them. I wished that I was strong enough to make things better, but I had to stay focused on my own well being. There was not much I could do lying in a hospital bed. I could only hope that it all would work out in the end.

Over the next few days I started to feel better. Finally, the weekend arrived. This time my sister and I had a wonderful visit. I felt better and better each day. She tried to reach Brian, but he had become unavailable. She reassured me that I should let him cool off and wait until I got home to deal with it. I agreed that that was the best thing to do. The night before my sister left, she stayed with me till almost midnight and we talked and laughed about old times. We had a wonderful time.

A few days later, I got to go home. A biopsy was performed before I went home, and no more leukemia cells were found. This was my last treatment. As soon as I got home, I changed my clothes and went to see my son's high school principal. He pulled him out of class and we discussed the problems Brian had been having. Brian agreed to come back home after school. I rushed back home and got ready to see my daughter's first spring concert at her grade school with my husband and his parents. I wanted to be there for her, also. It had been an exhausting day.

Chapter 4

Life Goes On

*Everything in life happens
for a reason.*

I made an appointment a week later to see my oncology doctor one last time. It seemed I would have to switch doctors because my insurance company had gone bankrupt. I did not find this out for several weeks. My husband had found out the company had gone bankrupt the day I was put in the hospital. He was in total shock. My coverage would be canceled effective on my due date, which was in April. Since my new insurance company was an HMO, I could only go to their doctors and hospitals. It seemed so unfair. I was just glad I had finished all my chemo treatments.

The doctor and I said our good-bye's and I gave him a big hug and thanked him for all his help. He truly is a great, devoted doctor. I will never forget what he has done for me. I said good-bye to all his nurses and gave each one a big hug. I gave Jan an extra hug for being there for me when I was first diagnosed. They were all very good listeners. I knew that I would miss everyone, and we promised to keep in touch.

The next day, my husband and I went to Madison to see the transplant doctor. We discussed a transplant at the University Hospital. He believed that the bone marrow transplant should be done right away. I knew that my sister was a match, but I decided not to do it right then. I needed to go back to my family and be an active family member again. I told the doctor at University Hospital to get everything ready and just put the transplant on hold for now. If the leukemia were to come back, I would have no other alternative but to have it done. I felt really good and didn't want to be in the hospital again right away. They respected my wishes, but advised that the bone marrow procedure would be in my best interest, since the odds of the leukemia coming back a second time were great. I wanted to take my chances. I thanked them for all their help and said that I hoped that I wouldn't have to see them again under those circumstances.

The next day, I had a meeting with my new oncology doctor. He seemed like a very nice person. He checked my charts and said that my counts all looked good. I only needed to come back once a month to the lab and get my blood drawn; I didn't need to see him unless my counts started to go back down. I thanked him for his help.

I tried to get on with my life as normally as possible and put everything behind me. The week after I got out of the hospital, I went back to check on my office. It was tough to handle so soon after everything— but it was good therapy for me. I felt strong and normal after everything I had been through.

Before I left the hospital, the staff encouraged me to join a therapy group. I decided to check it out. The session took place in the basement of my previous oncology doctor's office. Two women, a social worker and the hospital chaplain initiated the informal meeting. The seating was in a semi-circle. They reassured those of us in the group that we did not have to talk if we did not want to. Whatever was comfortable to us was OK. We did, however, go around and state our names. If we wanted to reveal our disease and talk about it, we could do so in a confidential way. I don't know what it is about getting together with strangers and talking about your private life; maybe there is a sense of safe haven about it, since they do not know you or your family.

I distinctly remember a pretty red-haired girl, a few years younger than myself. I immediately felt a bond with her. She was quite depressed because of her disease, and at the time I wanted so much to help her and give her strength, but I didn't know how. I guess I just wasn't ready yet to handle it. I couldn't even handle myself yet. After the session, the girl and I walked out together, side by side. We never said anything to each other, but I felt an incredible energy inside as I walked beside her. I felt it bouncing off both of us. There definitely was an invisible bond between us that I really can't explain.

That was the last time I went. I decided not to go back. I wasn't ready for this yet. I don't know why, but I thought going to a therapy group was a sign of weakness. (My ego again.) I can handle my own problems myself, I thought at the time. I would come to regret this decision.

I began having numerous hot flashes. It felt as if my whole body was on fire. It was so unpredictable. I didn't understand what was happening to me and thought the leukemia was back. I went out to dinner with a friend and I became so hot that I had to go outside. She explained to me that it could be the first sign of premature menopause. I wish someone had told me about this, since I had no idea what menopause symptoms were. She gave me a book to read and explained it all to me. Her mother had just gone through it after receiving chemotherapy treatments.

It was now the middle of summer and I was still a little paranoid about germs. I used my sleeves to hold public doors open so I didn't touch them with my bare hands. I always washed my hands before putting anything in my mouth. Food would always stick to my teeth, so I always had to carry toothpicks. I bought all kinds of wigs: long, short and different shades. I decided to have fun with them. My friends couldn't wait to see what I had on next. My hair finally started growing back in August. It came back thick, dark brown, and curly. By fall, I had a pretty good set of hair.

Rick and I had to go to a wedding in Indiana with my friend Debbie and her husband Mark. Rick and I stood up for their wedding, with Rick being Mark's best man. We decided to get a hotel room and spend the weekend. It was so good to go do something pleasant for a change.

A few weeks later, my husband's employer informed the staff that he was retiring and closing the business. Rick would be permanently laid off. This was the first time he had not worked since he was eighteen years old. He decided to become a "Mr. Mom" for awhile. He realized it wasn't all that bad and really enjoyed the experience. I went to the office every day and he stayed home and took care of the household. We also thought it would be good for him to learn all he could about my license and title business. So he came in to the office a few hours a week so that he could come to comprehend the whole procedure. I knew it would be quite easy for him, since he had been working in financing most of his life.

Rick has been so wonderful throughout this whole ordeal. He never once complained about anything. Thank God for a wonderful, supportive family. I couldn't have done it without all of them by my side. I hope, someday, I will be able to hold my grandchildren.

I started to go back to the bookstores in search of other books, trying desperately to find the true meaning of life. I read another interesting book about spiritual guides or angels, as some would call them. We have many spiritual guides to connect with our higher self that can give us guidance in life. There are people in this world called "mediums." These are people who have powers of communicating with other spirits. There is also one mentioned in the Bible. The first book of Samuel, Chapter 28, refers to this medium. Saul wanted a medium to bring forth the spirit of Samuel to find out why God was no longer communicating with him. Through the Witch of Endor's voice, Samuel told Saul of his fate fighting with the Philistines. It also was ironic that Samuel himself drove out all the mediums off his land and had to see this woman disguised. Talk about a hypocrite.

I also bought the books *Life Wish* by Jill Ireland and *Its Always Something* by Gilda Radnor. I wanted to learn how they had coped. Dr. Bernie Siegel's books and Louise Hay's books were also on the top of my list to read. I was becoming a bookworm.

I had also been feeling like I wanted to help others in my position. I started meeting with other patients in the hospital to give them encouragement. I hoped to reflect my very positive, fighting attitude unto them. It was so rewarding to me. My first patient was a middle-aged German woman. She spoke with a very heavy German accent. She was so frightened. I tried to comfort her as best as I could. She got better and left the hospital.

The oncology nurse called me again a couple of weeks later to talk to another patient. She was about my age, married with two small children. I tried to talk to her with a positive attitude, but I felt that she wasn't interested. She was so angry over her condition. I left disappointed. A few months later, she died. My husband and I decided to go to the funeral home and pay our respects. I thought I could handle it, but I had no idea of the reaction that I would have. As we got closer and closer to the casket, I started to panic. I looked inside and saw her lying there. Tears ran down my cheeks. This could have been me. Why did I live and she had died? I managed to get through the family line and they told me that I had brought her a lot of comfort when I visited her. I thanked them with a nod, too choked up to speak. But I hadn't saved her. Maybe if I had helped her more–had gone to see her more–I felt so helpless. I almost felt like it was my fault. I also started to think of the red-haired girl and wondered how she was doing and why I hadn't helped her yet. I knew we could become good friends and help support one another. I went into a deep depression.

I realized that I had to get all my feelings out. I had put up a brick wall in the beginning and had thrown my emotions over it. I had not yet taken that wall down. So the next night, I got myself a bottle of wine. I told my husband that I was going to stay up late, after everyone was safe in bed, to sort out all my feelings. He had no complaints. That night I let that brick wall come crashing down. I cried and cried and let each emotion come out. I finally realized what I had been through. I was never to be the same again. I will always be the different one from all my friends. I had to accept that. I still wanted to help others. Maybe that's my destiny.

I thanked God for giving me my life back. I watched the beautiful sunrise and listened to Mother Nature wake up. It was a beautiful sound. I felt so peaceful. I climbed into bed and felt relieved. It was over. Now it was time to try and put everything behind me.

A few weeks later, I received an unexpected phone call from my girl-friend, Mary, who had given me "Therapy." Her husband, Ray, had died unexpectedly. He was best man in our wedding. Rick took the news very hard. We were in a daze for days. I had first met Ray when he moved in with Rick and I when we lived in Milwaukee. He had come from Indiana. He only lived with us for a short time, until he got his own place. But during that short time he was with us, we became good friends and had always stayed close throughout the years. We had already moved to Rockford when Ray called and wanted us to meet his new girlfriend, Mary. We decided to meet in Lake Geneva, Wisconsin, for the weekend.

The rest is history. Mary and I were the same age and of the same mold. Our friendship grew close. So, I tried to help her out and comfort her as much as I knew how in this time of need. I also wondered if our friendship would fade away. But I will never forget after the funeral, we both hugged and agreed to always be close, no matter what. I decided to let her have "Therapy" to help her get through the tough times, just as he had helped me. And if I were to fall on tough times again, she would send him back. Our friendship grew stronger from that moment on.

My family decided to come down for Thanksgiving for the first time ever. It was a wonderful gathering. I decided to have a Christmas party that year and invited all my friends and neighbors. I wanted to celebrate and be grateful I was still alive. Rick and I went out and celebrated New Year's Eve with our close friends. It was a night to remember. I recalled that I had entered the hospital on this day last year. I was thankful that it was in the past, or so I thought.

Chapter 5

The Leukemia Is Back

You cannot change tomorrow
until you change today.

As I write this chapter, it has been over a year since my last treatment. I have dyed my hair back to blond. My period has come back and the hot flashes have left. Having gotten pretty much back to my original self physically, I wanted my life to change so that it would have more meaning, but I didn't know how to bring this about. I started to get confused about the whole thing. Psychologically, I found myself slipping back into my old ways and bad habits. I was mad at myself for my weakness. I let stress back into my life again. I also started to go a hundred miles an hour, always rushing and not taking time out for "me." My business wasn't a challenge to me anymore. I felt myself getting bored. I wanted to seek a new adventure, but I couldn't come up with any plan. Rick was also working full time again, putting in numerous hours. I was so exhausted after work, I didn't have much time to spend with my children. We were right back to where we had been before I got sick. I was miserable.

On the Fourth of July weekend, my husband and I and another couple decided to go up to Milwaukee and spend the weekend at Summerfest. Summerfest is a weekend of fun. They have numerous musical bands, food, rides, and shops. The event is right on the shore of Lake Michigan. We first started going years ago with Ray and Mary. As the years went by, the group of friends that came with us grew and grew. We would always get a picnic table at one of the stages and just have a great time. We would get hotel rooms and a group of us would go from morning until late at night. But as we got older, life changed. We all now have families and other interests and had gone our own separate ways.

So here we were, once again. I wasn't sure if I really wanted to go. But, I knew that Rick did, and he deserved to have fun–especially after all he had been through with me. We arrived at the hotel, unpacked and arranged for a cab to drive us to Summerfest. At the festival, I started to get irritable and sluggish in the middle of the first day. By evening, I was exhausted. I couldn't wait to get back to the hotel and just crawl into bed and sleep. In the morning, we got up and started all over again. Within an hour of being there, I found myself already worn out. Once again, I felt the old familiar clammy feeling. Then it hit me. The leukemia was back. I kept my feelings to myself, not wanting to spoil it for everyone, and managed to get through the rest of the weekend.

On Monday morning I called the clinic to set up a CBC for the next day. I emotionally started to prepare myself. My new oncology doctor called me at the end of the week to say that a biopsy would be performed on Monday to determine if the leukemia was back. The CBC revealed that my blood count was down. I asked him when I would have to go into the hospital, if it was back. The results wouldn't be back until Thursday, so probably the week after, he answered. Then I asked him the strangest thing. I wanted his approval to go on a mini-vacation next weekend before I entered the hospital. He told me to go and to have a good time.

After I got off the phone, I walked into a travel agency and asked if there were any weekend vacation flights to Cancun, Mexico for that next weekend. As luck would have it, there was one scheduled to leave the following Thursday and return on Sunday.

I had always been fascinated by ancient history. To this day I cannot explain it, but at that time it was important for me to see the ancient ruins of the Mayans before I went into the hospital. I decided to book a flight for two. I had never done anything like this in my life, on the spur of the moment. I hadn't even told my husband about the bone marrow biopsy, let alone the weekend trip.

I can't imagine the look on his face when I hit him with this! When I arrived home, I sat Rick down and informed him about my blood count. I needed to go have a biopsy done next week. He was in shock. I also blurted out about the Cancun trip. He looked at me like I was out of my mind. He couldn't believe the leukemia could be back and that we would have to go through the hospital thing all over again. He was really puzzled that I even had a vacation planned, on top of it. The poor man was totally confused. He began to get very upset with me. He refused to go on a vacation just on the spur of the moment, since he had recently started a new job. He wondered how could I think of such a thing at this time. I begged him to understand. This might be my last vacation. I explained to him that I had the doctor's approval. Rick had many questions. How to tell my boss? What to do with the children? What about taking care of the business? What if the leukemia wasn't back? Mexico is too hot this time of year.

I had answers to all of his questions. Everyone and everything would be fine. They would all manage without us for a few days and survive. I had already made plans for someone to look after them. I finally convinced him to go along with my crazy plan.

On Monday morning, I arrived at the doctor's office. We did the bone marrow biopsy and discussed my trip. He agreed with me wholeheartedly that I should go on this trip. I needed the encouragement.

The doctor was to call me with the results Thursday morning before I left. I was so excited about my trip that it kept my mind off the transplant for the next few days. On Thursday morning, the doctor called and confirmed that after I had gone fifteen months of being leukemia-free, it was back. He told me to go on my vacation and have a good time—but when I came back, I must prepare to enter the hospital for the bone marrow transplant in Madison.

I called my husband with the bad news. We had both agreed the night before, if it was back, that he would quit his job and take over my business. I also called my sister and told her the bad news. She would have to be the donor after all. When I told her about our Cancun trip she didn't say much, but I was sure that she was just as confused as my husband had been.

I called my mom and also told her the news. I urged her not to worry. I called the hospital in Madison and obtained the details. I would need to come in early Tuesday after my trip to start the transplant. They wanted me there on Monday, but I refused. I needed Monday to be with my children when I got back. Everything and everyone was all set. Within a few hours, we arrived at O'Hare Airport.

We landed in Cancun early Thursday evening. I was so excited to be there that my energy level seemed to be strong. As we got our luggage, I realized that I was having a hard time breathing. It was so muggy. I kept it to myself and made myself get used to it. (It's amazing what you can do once you set your mind to it.) We arrived at our hotel, checked in, and started to explore the place. I put the transplant out of my mind and decided to enjoy this vacation to the fullest. We tried to do everything there is to do in the city that night and the following day.

On Saturday morning, I traveled to the ancient city, Chichen Itza, with a tour group. My husband decided to stay at the hotel and relax. After a long bus ride we finally arrived. I was so excited, I couldn't wait to get out of the bus. The tour guide escorted us through the jungle onto a pathway, entering the ancient city. He explained the ruins and the odd cool weather to us. It had been scorching hot all summer. This was the first day the weather had been nice, even with a breeze. I waited impatiently for him to stop lecturing. There was limited time, and I wanted to explore the entire place on my own.

At last, I faced the El Castillo pyramid and stared at the steep stairs. In a trance-like state, I started to climb to the top. I stood up there at the temple and felt a strong sense of ecstasy. You can view all the ancient ruins in their splendor. I felt at peace. Coming down, I touched the head of the beast, which is supposed to help the sick. Somehow I felt that everything would be okay. I also wanted so much to climb the stairs inside the pyramid. I walked up about twenty stairs that are very narrow and steep. I was having such a hard time breathing that, with great disappointment, I had to turn back. I would have to come back here again someday. I started to walk around the big outdoor city. I walked over and stared at the walls of skulls. They had the effect of putting me in a trance. I was so intrigued. I looked at my watch; it was time to go already. I would miss this place, but never forget the emotional feeling I experienced.

On the last night in Cancun, Rick and I went out to dinner and talked seriously about the future. It was time to unwind and get ready for the big event. We went back to the hotel early. I tried to get some peaceful sleep before facing reality.

As we were in the airport the next day waiting for our flight home, I started to look for something in my purse and found a pack of cigarettes. I had never been a hard-core smoker. I usually went through a pack of cigarettes in a week. I was more of a social smoker. I took them out of my purse and said good-bye to them forever, and threw them in the trash. This was the first real change in my life.

We arrived home early Sunday evening. The house hadn't burned down. All the children were well. Everything and everyone was fine. On Monday morning I started to prepare to go into the hospital. I didn't even have time to think about it or to be scared. There was too much to do. I started the laundry that had piled up over the weekend and found out my dryer was on the fritz. I immediately called a repair service and explained my situation. The repairman arrived within the hour and fixed the problem. I will always be thankful to him. I packed my things and got ready for the next day.

We called Rick's parents and they said they would be down to pick up Nikki and Chris to take them back to Michigan. My sister and mother decided to stay in Madison after the transplant for a week to give me support. They were to arrive at the end of the following week.

I gathered all my children together. They would have to be brave, stick together and help each other out. I spent a close, quiet night with my family. I assured them that I would be back, and I meant it. I tucked my little Ally to bed. I started to read her favorite bedtime book to her, as I do every night. She took the book and said that she would read it to me tonight, because I needed it more. She knew the words by heart. I told her how much I loved her and that she will always be in my dreams. She gave me a big kiss goodnight and told me to have sweet dreams.

Chapter 6

Bone Marrow Transplant

Death was calling me again.
I put it on hold.

On July 20, 1993, I arrived at the hospital at approximately 8:00 a.m. and went directly to Admissions, then straight to Pulmonary Functions. This is where you blow into tubes that measure your lung capacity. I then proceeded to my room and met my nurse and doctor, who seemed very nice, and other people I don't remember. The room was very small and gloomy. I had one closet that was so small; I could barely get anything into it.

I was wheeled to x-ray so that my teeth and chest could be checked. Then it was off to the ear, nose, and throat specialist, and on to the eye doctor. They also did an EKG (ultrasound on my heart). Then on to radiation therapy to give me information on the procedure. I felt as if I'd been on every floor and elevator in the hospital that day. I was already getting very familiar with the place. Finally, I went back to my room just in time to go to the bathroom and rush off to the MUDG testing. This test is when they take blood and mix it with radiation, then put it back, and do some tests on the results. I also went to physical therapy and had some physical tests to determine my strength. Next it was back to my room, where a nurse was waiting to insert an IV in me. It was almost 8:00 at night and I still had to go down to get a CAT scan. Every time I left my hospital room for a procedure or test, I had to be pushed in a wheelchair.

I arrived back at 11:45 and finally crashed in bed. I hadn't even had time to call the family. The next day there were people in and out of my room beginning at 6:00 a.m. I tried to go back to sleep. By 8:00 a.m. my nurse was waking me up. I had to get ready for surgery by 8:30. I jumped out of bed and into the shower. I had half of my makeup on and wet hair when they came to get me for surgery. They put tubes in me again and this time give me "happy medicine." This tube is called a Hickman catheter. It is inserted like the Groshong, but this one has three ports instead of just two. I felt real good until later, when nausea set in.

In the afternoon they did a spinal tap and gave me more "happy medicine." This time I just slept till 5:00 p.m. The nurse came in and hooked me up to the chemo machine ("Fred"). I decided to get up and explore the hospital. I went down into the gift shop and got a present for my stepdaughter, whose birthday is a day after mine. I bought her a plaque that reads:

> *When things go wrong as they sometimes will,*
> *when the road you're trudging seems all uphill,*
> *when the funds are low and the debts are high,*
> *and you want to smile, but you have to sigh,*
> *rest if you must, but don't you quit.*
> *Life is queer with its twists and turns,*
> *as every one of us sometimes learns,*

and many a fellow turns about
when he might have won had he stuck it out.

Don't give up though the pace seems slow—
you may succeed with another blow.
Success is failure turned inside out
the silver tint of the clouds of doubt,
and you never can tell how close you are,
it may be near when it seems so far;
so stick to the fight when you're hardest hit,
It's when things seem worst that you mustn't quit.

Author Unknown

She had been going through some rough times, so I hoped this would help. The plaque also gave me strength just reading it. Once back in my room, I put my pajamas on and started to call family and friends. Since the hospital was about 100 miles away from my home, it was hard for them to come visit everyday. I also called a woman who had lymphoma and had undergone a bone marrow transplant one year ago. I had talked to her a few times about it before and she had given me some insight on the procedure.

I slept like a baby. It was July 22. I awoke at 8:00 a.m., just in time for the doctor's daily visit. I ate breakfast and showered, and took my walk up and down the halls. A few minutes later, Rick, my four kids, my mother-in-law and father-in-law came in together singing happy birthday to me. The nursing staff and my mother-in-law each brought me cakes. Anna, an old classmate of mine who lives in the area, entered carrying a balloon. It was a wonderful surprise. We all had cake and spent the whole day together. My family and friends also called and wished me a happy birthday. I gave Nikki her present and told her to open it the next day for her birthday. Rick's parents were to take Nikki and Chris

replaced by her immune system, and it was expected that she would feel a little tired until it fully rejuvenated.

Rick and my close friend Debbie showed up the next day. She brought her camcorder. Brian and my mom were also there. That morning I walked down to the gift shop to buy a balloon and present for my sister. For some reason I had lots of physical and emotional energy.

My sister came out of surgery and was put in a room close to mine. We all gathered in her room and waited for the bone marrow to be processed. She was doing just fine, but was a little sore. I went back to my room for a private moment and meditated.

This is it. I get another chance at life, and this time I will not blow it. I played the song *Beat It* on my earphones before I got infused with my sister's bone marrow. My adrenaline started to pump. I had immense energy inside of me that just wanted to burst out into the open. I envisioned the theme song of *Rocky* going on in my head as I walked down the hall. I felt energy surge in and out of my body. It was such a tremendous power! I gave my sister a little speech about how grateful I was to her for giving me back my life. I gave her some gifts, a small token of my appreciation, and we gave each other a big, emotional hug. The nurse brought in the bone marrow. It just looked like a bag of blood. My sister and I played *Scrabble* as they began to infuse me with her gift of life. Debbie recorded the whole scene. It only took a few hours to infuse. Then we just sat and waited until it started to work.

A few days after the transplant, I was surprised that I still felt pretty good. My son, Brian, went home with Rick and Debbie the day of the transplant. My mom and sister came to visit me everyday and stayed till dusk. We took walks, did puzzles, went out on the hospital terrace, and just enjoyed each other's company. A resident doctor from Iceland saw me every morning before my doctor arrived. He reminded me of the actor Liam Neeson, who starred in *Schindler's List*. I liked talking to the doctor and finding out about his country. The infectious disease doctor came in right afterwards. He checked my body to make sure no infections were starting to develop. After he left, in came the mail. I had received a letter from Allison, my seven-year-old daughter. She told me that she loved me and she prayed to God every night that she would still have a mom when she got home from Grandma's. She also had colored me a picture of a little girl helping out a small bird in need. (Allison's nickname is "Bird".) Tears started to form. It was so emotional. I made a vow that I would get well to be around to raise my children. I also received a package from one of my classmates. In it was a Get-Well card signed by all my classmates. I also received the class picture and information on each one. It made my day. How thoughtful of everyone; I will always be grateful.

By the end of the week, I was beginning to feel weaker and weaker. My sister and mom left for home the next day. I started to feel very miserable. My strength was nearly gone. When blood counts drop to zero, your life is no longer yours. You are kept alive with enormous amounts of drugs through this gruesome stage. They give you drugs for everything. It amazed me. I had started to get a temperature real bad in the morning, and by the afternoon I was so cold that my teeth were chattering. My heart hurt from shaking so much. The nurse came in to check on me and noticed my trembling. She left at once and came back and gave me an injection. Almost immediately, the chills stopped and I was back to normal. No more "Shake and Bake." She advised me that if it happened again, to call a nurse instantly so they could give me the drug Demerol to stop it.

Now, I really liked my primary nurse and we got along quite well, and she did a good job. My secondary nurse was very good. She was very thorough, efficient, and authoritative–qualities that were really needed on that floor. When you are very sick like this, you need very good nurses to take care of you 24 hours a day.

However, the weekend nurses were dreadful. When my nurses went home for the weekend, I would get a sick feeling. If I'd ring for them during the night, they'd take their sweet time. One night I was in *so* much pain, and I desperately needed pain medicine. It took them one hour to get back to me. One weekend nurse insisted on weighing me at precisely 5:00 a.m. every morning. She just barged into my room, shook me, and commanded me to get on the scale. I was not much for complaining, but after a few weekends of that I started to complain to my day nurses. They fixed the problem.

Then one day an angel of a nurse stepped into my room. I have never met such a warm, sensitive, and caring nurse. Gail was there for me at my worst times. Whenever she came on duty, I felt an immense sense of relief. She went the extra mile, way beyond the call of duty. I even felt a little jealous when I found out that she treated all of her patients that way. I thought it was just me she treated so well. What a gifted nurse she was.

My doctor, a brilliant man who really knows his profession, is someone who I would describe as very kind and thoughtful and who is always on top of things. We got along very well; he usually visited me every afternoon. I felt safe and secure to be in such good hands.

Outside visitors were rare at this time. If someone visited, they would need to scrub their hands and arms and would have to wear a mask upon entering my room. I would rather not have had anyone see me in my condition, anyway, and the scarcity of visitors also helped to keep the infections out of my room. Someone else's cold could immediately have turned into pneumonia for me. That is why no one can come into your room sick. The lady with lymphoma came to visit a few days later, but I could hardly remember what we talked about. I must have been on

morphine at the time. Everything was a blur. I even started to hallucinate during the next couple of days.

On August 14th, I was still very weak. My girlfriend Mary came to
visit and brought *Therapy* back to me to help me get through the lonely
nights. She didn't stay long. I wasn't much company.

The next two days were also a blur. Fever, chills, nausea, headaches
and constant diarrhea had become part of my life. I tried to find my way
to the bathroom but gave up. The next day I started to feel a little better
and took a walk down the hall, but I barely made it back. I slept very
well today, still being so very weak. I began to notice that a lot of the
patients I knew had left the hospital. I would miss Sister Claire; she
always brightened everyone's day. The other patient who had a transplant a week after mine was having a very hard time, but was hanging in
there, like me. His wife and daughter were always by his side. He'll make
it, I thought; he's a determined man. Rick's mom and dad visited after
they had taken Allison home. (They didn't want to stop at the hospital
with Ally because my appearance and condition would have horrified
her.) I think my appearance alarmed them.

Although I barely remember it, my mother-in-law said I was shaking
when they arrived in my room, wearing masks. She held my hand and
sat beside me, trying to comfort me. My doctor came in and asked if I
could hang on until the next morning to take something for the shaking. I said I could. Later that night, my doctor came in and gave me
something for the shakes. I asked, "Why now and not tomorrow?" He
said, "I saw the fear in your mother-in law's eyes and wanted to reassure
her you would be okay."

Ice-chips were the only nourishment I could endure, and became a
lifeline for me. I could no longer eat the nauseating food. So they
hooked me up to a liquid diet. My husband tried to come by as often as
he could on the weekends and sometimes on weeknights. Otherwise, I
had no visitors.

One day I grew very restless. I didn't want to be in the hospital anymore, but I knew that to leave would be physically impossible. I put on my headphones and played one of the soothing tapes I had received. I tried to visualize a happy, carefree time in my life. My family and others once had owned a cottage on a lake when I was small. My immediate family, other relatives, and close friends used to go there every Sunday. It was a wonderful time in my life. I closed my eyes and envisioned that I was standing on the dock, looking at the cottage. Suddenly it came alive in my mind. I saw myself at about 10 years old, wearing an ugly one-piece plaid bathing suit. I had a pageboy haircut and lots of freckles. I could hear the other children and myself laughing and jumping into the water. I felt as though they went right through me while I stood on the dock. I watched as each one of us played in the water. I could hear the mothers chatting in the cottage. I took a deep breath and smelled the aroma of spaghetti sauce. I watched as some of the fathers play an Italian game. My father was standing near a homemade brick fireplace, cooking sausages. I could hear him laughing, talking and just enjoying the wonderful, relaxing day. One friend was merrily playing the accordion, while some tried to dance. I smelled the fresh, clean air of the outdoors. These memories lingered in my mind and gave me peace and comfort throughout the night.

A few days later I was allowed to go out of the hospital for a couple of hours in the car. I wore my wig and put on some make-up. (I had lost my hair again. I didn't have much to lose, so it was not that dramatic this time.) I couldn't wait till Rick and Ally got there. I was thrilled to see them. I put my mask on, and off we went. We drove around town, stopped at the lake and took some pictures. It felt so good to be let out. We stopped at McDonalds. My doctor had advised me to stay away from crowds, but my mouth was watering for a cheeseburger. After I had eaten it halfway through, I shrieked and threw the sandwich back in its box. I explained to Rick that I had eaten a sandwich with lettuce and tomato on it. I wasn't supposed to eat any vegetables that came from the ground. I started to panic. What if I was to get sick from this little mistake? I couldn't bear the thought of having to stay in the hospital any longer. As soon as we got back, I discussed my agonizing dilemma with my doctor. He reassured me that my blunder should not be a problem and said not to worry, and that I would be just fine. What a relief I felt.

When we got back to my room, the cleaning lady came in and started to clean. Rick noticed that she wasn't wearing a mask. We were very confused about this. I also didn't think it was a good idea for her to mop the floor with the same mop as was used in the other rooms. I was getting very paranoid about this. Rick finally approached the front desk and complained. They guaranteed him that they would take care of the problem.

Ultimately, the moment I had been waiting for finally arrived. My doctor came in and told me that I could go home by my sister's birthday if I had no fevers for three days and if I consumed enough calories. This might be a problem. I couldn't touch nor stand the smell of the food. The only thing I could eat was cereal out of a box. I had to think of a scheme. The nurse checked my plate at every meal to make sure I ate enough calories for the day. So I began to play with my food to make it look like I ate a lot and hid some of it wherever I could find a hiding spot. One time I attempted to start walking toward the bathroom to flush the soup down the toilet. The nurse walked in and asked where I was going. I acted confused and got back to the bed. I almost got caught. I would also go so far as to eat ice chips before they took my temperature, hoping it would read normal. I knew that once I got home, in my own environment, I would eat and crave my own food. Calories would not be a problem. Also, being home with my family would make me stronger and I would have that feeling of well being. I felt stronger just thinking about it.

Before I was discharged, I had to practice flushing out my tubes with heparin. The needle made me queasy. My nurse also instructed me on how to care of my Hickman by changing the dressing everyday. I did it several times during the day to get it right. I also had to remember to take my pills every day. I was told to stay away from crowds and anyone who was sick, keep company to a minimum and always wear my mask outside the house. The last night at the hospital was filled with excitement and anxiety. I could not sleep all night. I was so afraid my temperature was going to be high the next morning that I was making myself sick. But I managed to pull it off and got to go home August 25, 1993, the day before my sister's birthday. My doctor had kept his promise.

Chapter 7

The Journey Begins

Healing thyself takes patience.

That morning, I telephoned Rick with the good news. He arrived at the hospital so fast, I thought he had flown in. We anxiously waited a few hours for the release forms to be completed before we could leave. In the meantime, the pharmacist entered my room and explained all my prescriptions to me. The head nurse from the transplant clinic arrived and discussed my visits. I was to be required to come back every Tuesday for the next 100 days. Close monitoring of my blood chemistry, fluid balance, and hematologic (relating to blood and blood-forming tissues) status would be checked, and a nurse would administer drugs into my IV to prevent graft versus host disease and blood transfusions, if necessary. A few moments later, the nurse strolled in with my freedom papers. I was out-of-there!

The ride on the way home felt like I was on another planet. I hadn't been on a freeway for five weeks. It seemed like years. I couldn't wait to pull in the driveway and see my children when they came home from school. I missed them so much. As I walked in, I noticed how bare our sunroom looked without my plants. Rick had to get rid of all the plants in the house and disinfect the whole house before I came home. Also, we had just adopted two kittens that we decided to give away. They could not be in the house with me for six months after I came home. I was not allowed to be around anyone who was sick in any way and I could not eat or touch anything that came from the ground. I was very vulnerable to infections.

Rick cooked one of my favorite meals. We all had a wonderful night together. It felt so good to sleep with my husband again. I felt like I was in a dream for a few days at home.

I remember my first morning. I couldn't wait to have a piece of toast with real butter on it. But to my surprise, I could not taste it. I was so disappointed. I had temporarily lost my sense of taste due to radiation treatments. I could not hardly taste any kind of food, nor could I drink milk, coffee or pop. Kool-aid and water were the only things I could drink for awhile. I remember it being 100 degrees outside and we did not have air conditioning at the time. The only thing I could do was go from the bed to the shower to the couch and back again. I had no energy for anything else. Walking to the bathroom took a lot of energy. My daughter would have her friends over to swim in the pool. I remember it being too overwhelming for me to have any kind of company. I so desperately needed my quiet and rest. I usually stayed indoors and slept most of the time. I remember I couldn't watch anything on TV that had violence in it. It was really weird, but anything upsetting on TV made my whole body feel real tense.

The weekend came and Brian was sleeping over at his friend's house and Rick had to stand up for a wedding. When he left, Ally started crying hysterically and wouldn't come in from the garage where she had said good-bye to her daddy. I mustered up all the strength I could find inside me and went out to comfort her. She did not want any part of me, only her daddy. At that moment, I began to realize how hard my illness has been on her. Daddy had made her safe in her little world. I understood her fear of getting close to me–fear that it might not last again. I hugged her and told her we could go watch her favorite movie, pop popcorn, and she and I could lie on the couch side by side like old times. She wouldn't have any part of it. I tried to coax her in but failed. She only wanted her daddy. I realized it had to be her decision. I told her that I would go back into the house and when she needed me, I would come and get her. It seemed like an eternity before I finally heard her very faint call for mom. I went back out and wrapped my arms around her as best I could and held her close. She decided she did want to watch her favorite movie, *Beauty and the Beast,* with me after all. We both walked into the house hand in hand and had a wonderful night. We ended up falling asleep together on the couch. I don't think she wanted to let go of me, and I didn't want to let go of her.

After about a week, I began to run some temperatures. I started to develop a cold-like cough and was not feeling well. When I went for my hospital checkup, which was always once a week for the first 100 days, I developed an alarmingly high fever. I was admitted to the hospital and diagnosed with pneumonia. The nurses also had to stick me with needles to get blood from my arms instead of my tubes to get a culture in order to find out what kind of pneumonia it was. I was not happy. They also pumped me with high doses of antibiotics, but the fever would not go away. I became weaker and weaker and drifted into a deep sleep. I remember actually floating out of the universe next to the stars, looking down upon the earth. It was so bright. It sure was a beautiful moment. I will never forget that peaceful, serene image. It took two weeks in the hospital before I started to feel better. My mom and sister spent the first week with me. Thank God they did, or I think I would have gone crazy. The type of pneumonia I had is known as cytomegalovirus (CMV). I had survived the most feared and deadly infection.

By the third week, I was released from the hospital, but had to have an IV antibiotic for several weeks at home to insure that the pneumonia would not come back. A nurse came to my house to show me how to use it. The medicine was in a round plastic ball that was carried in my pocket. It was attached to my IV for about an hour. After the infusion, I had to master flushing out the IV with a needle. I also had to master all my many different medications. I always wore my bra to stuff the tubes inside.

About two weeks after coming home, I decided to be brave and walk outside to the end of the driveway to get the mail. This was a big step, since I was so weak that it took a big effort to walk. I remember it taking me a long time just to get off the couch, out the door, and down the walk and back again. I would also try to walk up and down the basement stairs once a day to build up my strength.

I started to feel better in October and started to go to the grocery store. My days were usually spent getting the kids up for school and out the door, then taking a nap; getting up for lunch, maybe straightening up a little and then going back to napping before the kids came home from school. Evenings included fixing supper, doing dishes, and laying on the couch the rest of the night before bed. I also exhibited some very strange eating habits.

I suddenly developed a mammoth appetite and had cravings I couldn't control. I would eat at least three bowls of ice cream a day! I had to have the strawberries, cream and nuts on it, also. Then after that craving was satisfied, I would go into a chocolate frenzy. I would buy packages of candy bars and hide them all around the house; I could eat at least five a day. I would even lock myself in the bathroom to eat them so I did not have to share. I was very stingy with my candy bars. When Halloween came, I had to run to the store at the last minute, because I had eaten all the candy.

Eating three helpings of supper was normal to me. Everyone would be done eating and going about their business, and I would still be at the table, eating. Needless to say, I started to gain three pounds a week, not to mention a very round face and stomach to match. I could not fit into any of my clothes except stretch pants. I started to panic. It was getting out of control. I couldn't even look in the mirror at myself! I learned that the cause of this voracious appetite was the steroid drug, *Prednisone*. The doctor decided to decrease the medication, and as a result my appetite, stomach, and face diminished somewhat.

Just before Thanksgiving, I developed mouth sores called chronic GVHD (graft versus host disease). The sides of my tongue were raw and I had open blisters inside my cheeks. I had been feeling miserable and irritable and my nose was constantly running. I always had to have a bunch of tissues on hand. My nose ran almost non-stop when I ate. It could be embarrassing, especially when at a restaurant. Also, food stuck to my teeth and I always had to carry toothpicks with me. My lips were very dry and cracked. I would not leave home without my medicated Blistex.

During the next visit to the doctor, we decided to increase the Prednisone to help clear up the mouth sores. This is the medicine that gave me my round figure. I was a little disappointed, but the sores of the mouth outweighed the figure this time. I also got some numbing medicine for my mouth so I could eat in peace for a little while. My counts and everything else looked good. Since I had been out of the hospital, I had never needed any blood transfusions.

I decided to join a class at the YMCA. My girlfriend and I took a class on *cha chi*, which is an exercise for the mind as well as the body. I also started to exercise at home. I had been having some side effects being on the Prednisone. My left calf and knee continued to be very sensitive. Constipation and gas were also major problems.

I decided to try the support group thing again. I was so amazed at how different I felt this time! I felt stronger and more aware of my feelings. There was a support group leader, a wonderful, caring woman. Everyone in the room got a chance to talk if they wanted to. It was very casual and you could come in at anytime and feel at ease. These people were having the same problems as me, and they understood what I was going through. I felt honored to be in their presence. It was not at all what I had expected. These were very brave and positive people. Why hadn't I realized that the first time? I looked around and didn't see the red-headed girl. I wondered what had happened to her. I thought I had it bad until I listened to their stories! Some of these people were preparing to die. I remember one gentleman who only had about a month to live. He seemed at peace with himself and had learned to accept it. Somehow, I wasn't afraid anymore. I learned so much each time I went. I tried to go every week. One can make some wonderful close and dear friends.

January arrived, and I felt so warm and cozy in my house. I took wonderful naps every day. Rick was running the business so I could stay home to get well. He came home from work, cooked supper, cleaned, did laundry and the grocery shopping and never complained about it. He even became a better cook than I was. I still had the mouth sores, but not as bad. I started to take little walks by my house for exercise, and the tiredness diminished. I think my energy level was starting to flow back into my body.

I even tried to find a "medium" in the area and had to settle on a psychic. She was not very good. Nothing she said ever happened. I had gone to one out of curiosity just after I opened up my own business, just to see what they had to say. I didn't even get a chance to sit down before she already knew that I owned my own business. She thought it had to do with real estate, which it didn't. She told me a lot about myself that no one else knew. She also told me I was afraid of water and tried to figure out why. My husband and I had just built an inground swimming pool in our back yard. I didn't like that it was going to be ten feet deep. Even when we had our cottage, I would never go over my head in the lake. I remember when I came home from work and they had just finished digging the hole for the pool. I had looked out the patio window and gasped. I ran into the bathroom and locked myself in. I was scared to death of that big hole filling up with water. I couldn't understand my feelings. I had never come close to drowning, so I didn't know what my problem was. Even when the pool was done, I wouldn't go near the deep end for months. Finally, with a lot of coaching and coaxing, Nikki helped me jump in for the first time in the deep end. Feet first, of course. She was right there just in case I panicked and didn't come up. I was terrified. The psychic now knew why I was afraid. She said she had seen me go down with Atlantis. That could be a pretty good reason for my terror, but I don't know if I could accept the answer. I pondered about that for a long time. Reincarnation is a touchy subject. I wanted so much to talk to someone about all this, to hear the pros and cons about it, but my family and friends always gave me that "crazy" look. I started to keep everything to myself. It was difficult and frustrating to find anyone who would talk about it. No one seemed interested.

During February I had the most boring week of them all. It was too cold to go outside and take walks. I basically just slept a lot. I was feeling sorry for myself a lot. I needed to circulate. My son and I decided to go to a concert in Chicago to see the Eagles. It was great to go with him, since he also enjoys their music. There were a lot of generations there. We had a great time.

Rick's sister called me and we talked for a long time. She called me frequently during my ordeal, giving me encouragement. She informed me that Ally had prayed for me every night at grandma's house when I was ill. One night, she had sobbed uncontrollably, asking Grandma if her mommy was going to die. She so desperately wanted her mommy. I had tears rolling down my eyes when I heard about this. It must have been hell for her to handle all of this at such a young age. I remember when Madonna and Rosey O'Donnell were interviewed one time. You could see it in their eyes how much pain and sorrow they had suffered, losing their mothers at a young and vulnerable age. I decided that I would not let this happen to my little girl. She needed a mother to hug her, be there when she was ill and rock her to sleep, to sing her lullabies and nurture her into a beautiful young woman. I thought, "I want to be there when she walks up that aisle arm and arm with her father. It will be a glorious day!"

Unfortunately, my thought processes were not always so positive. We had another snowstorm, and I began to feel the walls closing in. I'd been thinking of death a lot, wondering if I was really going to make it. I had to prepare myself in some way just in case. But how does such a person do it? I called a funeral home and had someone come over and talk to me. My husband thought I was crazy. The man tried to sell me a burial plot. I realized this was a dumb idea and gave it up.

I tried the visualization audiotape once again. A vase immediately came to mind and I got startled. In the background, I noticed a tree with a lot of branches in a distance. The tree had no leaves and appeared to be dead. Someone or something was standing near it, wearing a long black cape with a hood. I could not see the face. I wasn't afraid, but I was really puzzled as to who it was. I tried to concentrate more, but couldn't. I gave up.

The day arrived when my sister and her family came down for the weekend. I had been very excited about this. We had a lot of fun. We stayed up as long as we could and got up early in the morning so as not to miss any precious time with each other. I wish she and her family could move down here by us. It was sad to see them go.

By the time March arrived, I had been feeling better and better physically. I needed to venture out of the house and mingle with other people. I had sheltered myself from everyone except my family. I even stopped going to support group. I was beginning to get depressed every day. I decided to visit my good friend, Karen. She has always been there for me to listen. I told her how I had been feeling. We had a wonderful conversation and she literally got me back on my feet again. She now calls me to make sure I'm okay. I have very dear friends. I started to explore museums, plays, and even symphonies. Making plans to go to lunch with friends once a month helped me to look forward to something. I seemed to feel better when I did this.

I finally went back to my support group. I built up enough courage to ask what had happened to the red-haired girl. The leader had told me that the girl had passed away, and she gave me a copy of a poem her mother had written about her. It was so beautiful and touching. I don't know why I felt so much emotion toward her. I wish I had been strong enough back then to be a close friend. We were both too shy, though. Even though I met her only once, I felt an inseparable attachment toward her. It was very mysterious.

Rick received a call from Nikki. She wanted to move down here with us, since she had just graduated from high school. We had Brian drive to Michigan and bring her down. The first week she was here, we hung out together, went places and settled in. Rick had her start at the office the following week. It kept her busy. I started to think that Brian was to graduate that year. I remembered my goal. I had to stay alive to see him graduate. That goal seemed to be coming true.

I now went to my doctor in Madison once a month. But on April fifth, my sensitive knee got worse. It started about 4:00 a.m. I started to get real sharp pains on the left side of my knee. By the morning I was in excruciating pain. I had to crawl to get to the bathroom. My husband had to open up the office that day and had to leave early. He called the doctor from the office and called to tell me to go to Madison that day. I had my son Brian and my stepson, Chris, take me. It was Easter vacation. It was also Brian's birthday. I laid in the back seat all the way to Madison, trying to keep my knee as still as possible. The doctor had to take fluid out of my knee and found out I had an infection in it. I couldn't believe this was happening to me. How could I have gotten TB in the knee? It was such a rare thing to happen. I didn't even know what it was till the doctor explained it to me. The strange thing is, I never had a cough and it wasn't in my lungs. He made me an appointment with the infectious disease doctor that same day. They put me on several different medications plus the ones related to the bone marrow.

I stayed in bed the rest of the week. The pain became unbearable. I wouldn't let anyone go near my knee. They gave me so much medication at first that I started to throw it all up. I started to become really ill, and I could hardly get out of bed. My sister called me at noon one day to see how I was. She became very angry. She called my bone marrow doctor and told him that the infectious disease doctor had given me several different medicines to take and that I couldn't keep anything down. He had a doctor here in town analyze the drugs and found out I only had to take two of the drugs for my infection, so we dropped the others. The next two days were hell. I must have had drug withdrawal. I had a temperature of 100.8. One minute I would be sweating and the next I would be freezing. I ached all over.

I then started to feel better in a week, and the pain was not so severe anymore. It had been a rough two weeks.

Chapter 8

Reality Sets In

Always find a goal to achieve.
When it has been met, find another.

During the month of June I was busy preparing for Brian's graduation. My stress level was pretty high. I worried that my goal was coming true and I needed to think of another one to replace it.

The graduation turned out fine. All the relatives were down and we had a big graduation pool party in the backyard. My mother stayed on for a couple days, and I decided to take her to a few places since she doesn't get out much. We went to a Phantom Regiment concert in the park. The Phantom Regiment is an excellent drum and bugle corps located right here in town. They have won several first place awards and are rated one of the top bugle corps in the country. I also drove my mom to Kenosha, Wisconsin where her brother lives. She hadn't seen him for quite a few years. We all had a very nice visit.

My knee was still painful in the morning. I usually took my pills and then went back to bed for a nap. I was still pretty much drowsy in the morning and didn't focus very well until about noon. Napping was still a big part of my life.

On June 20, I went to Madison for a checkup taking Mom, Brian, Chris and Ally with. Another drug was prescribed for the swelling of my knee. We then met my brother to take my mom home. We drove through Wisconsin Dells on our way back home. I had always wanted to go there but had never had the chance. Once I feel better, I want to do a lot of traveling. I want to see much as I can of this beautiful world of ours. I especially want to go to the Middle East. The Holy Land would be the ultimate trip.

Well, I colored my hair back to blonde again. I just couldn't get used to the dark hair. I was trying to get better, both physically and emotionally. It was a hard mountain to climb. Yesterday, my husband came home with a 1993 Ford Mustang convertible for my birthday. It is a beautiful car. I thought I was dreaming! He said I deserved it, with all I've been through.

My knee has been feeling better with taking Motrin so that I could actually put my leg down with force with no pain, but rather just a sense of pressure. I just had to work on my mouth. I didn't get the mouth sores in the hospital during the transplant like some patients, but paid the price later. I couldn't even brush my teeth or use toothpaste. My doctor told me to gargle with salt water, which is the best thing for mouth sores. I finally found a soft electric toothbrush. It worked wonders. My sister called me about melalelica oil or Austrian tea oil, which is supposed to help mouth sores. I was so tired of coping with the sores that I'd try just about anything. My mother-in-law sent me a bottle of natural herbs and plant ingredients to take by mouth every day. She swore by it. It helps to build the immune system. I started to take that and felt more energy by the end of the week.

I was benefited by a lot of my "power naps" at this time. This is when I would lie down and in a matter of minutes I would be in a deep sleep; I'd wake up fifteen minutes later, feeling refreshed.

A year ago today, I had entered the hospital for a bone marrow transplant. My sister and her family sent me a bouquet of balloons for the occasion. They are always so thoughtful. It sure went by fast. Glad it's all over, I hoped it would keep on working.

Brian moved out of the house, leaving me–as well as his room–empty. But somehow I knew it was for the best for him to go out and experience the world around him.

My second goal after Brian's graduation came true. I wanted my daughter to start taking piano lessons, and I bought an old upright piano for one hundred dollars that worked fine. It also cost me one hundred dollars to have it delivered! It was still a deal. We had fun playing on it.

Rick and I traveled to Madison for my check-up. They did the annual bone marrow biopsy. The doctor prescribed estrogen tablets for me to start taking. Every time I left after my appointments, I felt a surge of energy. I guess it was just a sign of relief that I was still okay. But on this day, I felt a sense of tension, awaiting the results for Friday. I couldn't imagine it being back, but you never know. The hour and a half trip back home exhausted me. The next day was spent sleeping.

I went to the store and picked up Lysine and acidophilus, two vitamins to help my mouth sores someone had told me about. My body felt so sore all over of a sudden. I felt as if someone had beaten me.

I got a call that my test results had come back normal–but I hadn't been feeling normal. My legs had been hurting more and more. I had chills, fever, and night sweats. I had headaches everyday and the pain was so severe that I had been spending lot of time in bed. I made an appointment to see my Madison doctor and he could not find anything wrong with me. He assured me that the AML was not back and go home and get lots of rest. So, I went and did just that. I stayed in bed the next few days, but still felt awful. The pain had become so unbearable that I could hardly get out of bed. Sometimes it felt like there were flies all over my body, constantly on me. It was such an uncanny feeling. I called my in-town doctor and explained how I felt. He said it didn't sound serious, but to wait and talk to my other doctor after the weekend. I felt so terrible, I didn't know what to do anymore. The night sweats were back, the chills and fever were there every night. I had been feeling bad with no relief in site. Then I remembered that I had started to feel this way just after I started the estrogen tablets. I called my mother and asked her about this. She too had gone through the chills, fever and night sweats for awhile and didn't use any hormones and just let it happen naturally. I immediately decided to stop the pills. I don't know why, but the menopause symptoms started after I took the pills and it was supposed to be the opposite. I just did not understand this menopause thing. In a few days, I started to feel normal. The leg pain, the chills, fever, night sweats and that "awful feeling" were all gone.

In October, I tried to go to the office for a couple of hours a day. By 5:00 p.m., I was totally drained but managed to go out to supper with Rick and Nikki. I coughed and blew my nose through the whole meal. Coming home, I took my temperature and it was 100.9. I went right to bed. The next few days I stayed in bed, feeling miserable. My lips stuck together and I had to pry them open. I looked in the mirror and saw that my eyes were all swollen, dry, and red. My head started to throb. I had been living on Motrin for the aches and pain. I hated to have to take painkillers every day to function. I just wanted to be normal. My stomach decided to join in with the misery. My right hand was swollen and puffy and I could no longer wear any rings. By the next day, I started to feel better. I just felt a little hazy and had a slight headache. I decided to go to my yoga class and take a nap as soon as I got home. My tongue was really hurting now. I looked at it in the mirror and saw that it was all swollen, red and seemed to be raw. The sores were also on my lips. It hurt so bad that I had to put a numbing medicine in my mouth and hurry up and eat before it wore off. By that night I felt a little better.

I hadn't gone to the support group lately and needed some comfort, feeling so sick. It was so nice to see everyone. They lift my sprits up. My leg hardly ached, my mouth didn't stick together, my bones didn't ache and I actually had energy. I felt really good about myself, and I hoped that the feeling would stay.

Rick and I decided to go out together and have a little time to our selves since I was feeling better. It was nice, but took a lot of my energy. My arms and legs had been getting numb off and on. I bought one of those plug-in massagers to circulate the blood. I used it on all my sore spots, especially on my neck and back. I felt so much better when I used it everyday. I started to take a good hard look at my body. I had very dry spots on my thighs and various other parts of the body. I also noticed that when I wore my watch, socks or tight pants, my skin seemed to hold the image of the imprint for awhile. I also had an itchy rash of little bumps under my arms and around my waist.

My girlfriend Mary from high school called me and said she was working in Madison for a couple of weeks and wanted to get together. So, I decided to drive up to Madison and spend the night. We also called Anna (another classmate who lived in Madison, the one that brought me the balloon in the hospital) to get together with us. I didn't care how bad I might feel. This opportunity would likely never happen again, with us three being together again, and I didn't want to miss it. It felt like we were in high school again. We had a great time. We talked and laughed about old times. My pain somehow didn't bother me that much on that trip. I wouldn't let it get in my way.

When I got home, my husband told me that the lady who had lymphoma had died. He knew about it before I left for Madison, but did not want to tell me about it at that time and ruin my weekend. I was in shock. She had been doing so well! She was two years past transplant. How could this happen. I started to sob uncontrollably. I felt like it was a setback for me, too. I needed to know what had happened, so I telephoned her family. She apparently had been sick for awhile and refused to go to the doctor or hospital until it was too late. By the time she was convinced that she should go, the pneumonia had set in the advance stages. I realized that I could not let this happen to me. If I were to get sick, I'd going straight to the ER.

My husband took a break from the office for a few days to go up north on a little vacation. I stepped in for him at the office. Nikki had decided to move back home, and now my son Brian had just started to work at the office. I was afraid that I wouldn't be able to do it but never let on. I barely made it through the week. I was so tired and exhausted by the last day. I stayed in bed the whole weekend.

I spent Thanksgiving relaxing and catching up on some sleep. I wanted to go 100 miles an hour and sometimes forgot that I was not a normal person. I had to realize that I couldn't run with the big dogs anymore and that my family would be there the next day. I couldn't wait. It would be fun and wonderful to see them again. Mary was still working in Madison, and I also invited her to come down. She was apprehensive to drive in the city, so we arranged to pick her up. Normally, Thanksgiving is very boring around here, but this year it was to be exciting. We had a very special time. My sister Joanne and I drove Mary back to Madison and stopped at the hospital to wish everyone a Happy Thanksgiving. The next day we all went shopping, which was my favorite thing to do.

On November 27th, Rick and I were at church. Our friends Debbie and Mark had asked us to be godparents for their second born, David. We were honored. She noticed that my eyes were really dry and suggested putting cortisone on them. It seemed to work.

Two days later, I went to Madison for my checkup. I now had a rash on my sides and under my arms. It itched constantly. My doctor said that it was chronic GVHD. Graft-versus-host-disease is a condition that occurs sometimes following a donor transplant. Immune cells in the transplanted marrow initiate an attack on body tissues of the recipient. In other words, my body saw my sister's marrow as foreign and tried to attack it. My system eventually died and my sister's strong marrow took over. But in the meantime, my system wouldn't leave without a fight.

The severity and extent of GVHD can vary. The areas affected by this disease are the skin, liver, and gastrointestinal tract. It can involve one or all three. So far, it was affecting only the skin. Immunosuppressive medications such as cyclosporine, methotrexate and Prednisone help to control this process. Since these drugs suppressed the immune system, serious infections can occur. My doctor increased the Prednisone to get rid of the mouth sores and help with the itching. He also had me start on estrogen creme. I still was not ready for the pills.

My insurance ran out at this time. After my husband was laid off from his job, I could only continue his insurance for fourteen months. Since no one else would take me, I would be on Medicare and on some kind of state insurance. This had been a real headache for my husband. The medical bills were astronomical.

During the two weeks before Christmas, I became very tired. I didn't know why, but I was feeling depressed. I didn't know if it was the Christmas blues. I hadn't been able to sleep much. We went to Green Bay for the annual Christmas get-together with my husband's family. That had been making me anxious and nervous. When we got back, Allison had her first piano recital. I was excited about that. Wednesday I had to make treats for the kids at school. I couldn't deal with everything. I was still too weak. One good thing was that the cortisone for my eyes had been working. They were not peeling anymore.

One day I took a nice warm bath, and noticed the dry spots on my legs seemed to be multiplying. By nightfall I couldn't sleep. I got up in the middle of the night and read the medical book on skin cancer. I read that there is a high risk for leukemia patients after bone marrow transplants. Just what, I didn't want to know. I grabbed a flashlight and shined it on one of the spots and flipped to the page where there was a picture of skin cancer and compared the two. I was getting worried. I thought about calling the doctor, but then it would have spoiled our holiday weekend and I was in limbo with insurance right then. I didn't want to put any more pressure onto my family, so I kept it to myself. I asked God to please tell me it wasn't so. I couldn't go through anymore. I pulled out the BMT booklet that the doctor gave me. The dry skin patches on my thigh seemed to be a common thing. What a relief! All that worry and loss of energy for nothing. I would have to stop doing that. Positive attitude!

Well, Christmas came and went. It's such a sad thing to say, but it had no meaning for me for some reason this year. It all seemed too commercialized. I think we have forgotten what it really is all about.

Using nyostatin in my mouth seemed to be working. One time I was baby-sitting for my godson and forgot my pain medicine. My mouth was so sore that I had to use a bottle of nyostatin for the baby for oral thrush, and it worked. It actually made my sores less painful. I had my doctor write me up a prescription for it. But the "dry spots" were getting worse. I now had one real bad, sore, dry spot at the bottom of my foot and on both sides of my feet under my ankles. They really were beginning to hurt. By the end of the day, my feet were really sore and pulsated with pain at night. I tried to get up in the middle of the night and take a bath in baby oil to try and soften up the dry sores. I spread lotion over my whole body. The lotion absorb instantly on my skin. This was to be another daily ritual. My hands were getting swollen. While I was in the office, an oriental man came in and noticed my swollen hands. He suggested boiling a piece of ginger root and drinking it as a tea every day, and the swelling should go down. I thanked him for his advice and after work I went to the grocery store and picked up some ginger root. I was getting desperate. I still use the massager every day to help me relax and feel better. It was my salvation. I was still taking Prednisone for my sores, and my mouth seemed to be healing. I ate my first McDonald's French fry on January 6, 1995 without it stinging my mouth. It had been over a year since I was able to do that. It was such a small thing, but I was ecstatic.

I sure do love life, despite my problems. I wake up every morning and feel so good to be alive. I especially love the days when I feel just about normal. I cherish the whole day. Only cancer patients can comprehend this feeling.

One day I came upon a box of letters and cards that I had kept from my hospital stay. I came across a letter from a stranger who had also gone through a bone marrow transplant in which her sister was the donor. She explained that she had a very hard time with it, but was doing fine now. She gave me a lot of encouragement. I sat down and wrote her a letter. She was from the same town as my sister. I didn't have her address so I called my sister to look it up. She paused for a moment on the phone and said she did not want to say anything before cause she didn't want to upset me, but the lady had died in November with pneumonia. I was first shocked and then decided not to dwell on it, but rather to go on with my life.

One day, I chose to get all dressed up and feel good about myself. I even wore my high heels. I enjoyed the day shopping. By bedtime my right leg was swollen and sore from the knee all the way to my toes. I was in pain most of the night. I sure paid the price just to look good!

Chapter 9

Severe GVHD of the Skin

It takes courage to live.

Graft-versus-host disease is a frequent complication of allogenic bone marrow transplants. In GVHD, the donor's bone marrow attacks the patient's organs and tissues, impairing their ability to function, and increasing the patient's susceptibility to infections. In fact, it is divided into two types of diseases called chronic or acute. Both chronic and acute GVHD can be a temporary inconvenience or a serious, life-threatening disease. In its severe form it started to attack one of my organs, the skin.

In the middle of February I was waking up with excruciating headaches. I tried some Motrin and relaxed using meditation techniques. This seemed to help a little. I also had this icky feeling all over that I can't quite describe and I would get very tired and irritable. I went to see my doctor in Madison to talk with him about how I felt and he told me that dry spots on my skin were from GVHD and that the swelling I was experiencing was from the dry spots pulling on my skin.

He explained that the condition was just temporary. After the visit I thought I would feel better like I normally did, but I was still feeling low.

The following day a scary thing happened to me. I tried to swallow a round Tylenol pill I took to relieve a headache. It got stuck in my throat and I couldn't breathe for a couple of seconds. I started to panic. Then, Rick walked in and saw me choking.

He immediately ran up behind me and gave me the Heimlich maneuver. It took three upward thrusts with his fists pressing hard into my abdomen and the pill literally popped right out of my mouth. Rick had saved my life.

As a result of this incident, I realized I was having difficulty swallowing. I would bite my pills in half so I could more easily swallow them and I was getting paranoid about swallowing anything. I wanted to resolve this problem at once so I called my oncology doctor to discuss my dilemma. He immediately set up an appointment with a gastroenterologist in Madison to perform an Upper GI Endoscopy, a test used to examine the esophagus, stomach and upper part of the intestine.

The test procedure involves passing a flexible viewing tube through the mouth into the stomach. The test results are used to find the cause of intestinal problems in order to treat symptoms, such as difficulty with swallowing. You are required to fast for six to eight hours prior to the exam. Since a sedative is used to perform the test, you must have someone else drive you home. (I had been driving myself to Madison for my appointments.)

In my case, it was learned that the esophagus had tightened and needed to be stretched so that it would be easier for me to swallow. Brian volunteered to come with me so he could drive me home. The first time the procedure was performed, I felt uneasy. An intravenous line (IV) was placed into one of my veins in my hand and a sedative medication was then administered just before the surgery. A local anesthetic was sprayed into the throat to make it numb. The test itself only took 15-30 minutes. After the exam, I was taken to the recovery room where I slept for about an hour. When I woke up I remembered nothing that had taken place and there was no pain or discomfort of any kind. The procedure went well. I could swallow safely again.

My leg was in pain once again. My skin started to feel like it was pulling and getting tighter and tighter on my body. The symptoms are related to a disease called scleroderma. It also relates to contractures, a shortening of a muscle, joint or skin. The skin feels like severe sunburn and I had to live with this inconvenience until the sensation burned itself out naturally. Thank goodness for pain medicine.

In May, I housed five Phantom Regiment girls. I admire their ambition and hoped some of it would rub off on me. They arrived on Memorial Day weekend. Everything they needed for their stay was downstairs, except for a kitchen. They only stayed for a couple of hours every day, basically to sleep. They worked gruesome hours in the hot heat. At the time I was not quite sure why I took this on, but I really enjoyed their company and they brought life into my home and gave me spiritual strength.

My husband and I decided to go into Chicago together for the day. We had a wonderful time. It was so good to get away from it all. The next day, I decided to go shopping for some clothes. I needed to buy some long dresses that would just hang on me. I never wore long dresses before, but my waistline seemed to get irritated when I wore anything tight or close to it. It was a beautiful day. I jumped in and put the top down on my Mustang and felt on top of the world.

When I got home, I felt a little funny, so I laid down. By the time I woke up an hour later, I felt worse. I was so hot I was starting to shake. I started to panic and cried, wondering what was so suddenly wrong with me. It came on so fast. I wondered if I had simply overdone it with all the activity or whether the leukemia was back with a vengeance. Allison had just come home from school and I told her I wasn't feeling so well and I was going to stay in bed. I didn't want to call Rick because I knew it was a busy day for him and thought I could hold on until he came home. I thought about calling the doctor but I wanted to wait and see if it went away. I took my temperature and saw that it was climbing. I did not want to go to the hospital. I begged it to go away, whatever it was.

Rick finally came home from work and took one look at me and knew I was in trouble. He tried to comfort me as much as possible. I stayed in bed the rest of the night. By 9:00 that evening my temperature had gone down. I felt a little relieved and fell asleep. By 5:00 the next morning, my temperature had shot up to 103.8 degrees.

I suddenly remembered what had happened to the lymphoma lady. Rick called my Madison doctor. He said we should go immediately to the emergency room and he would notify my oncology doctor in Rockford of my arrival. I was so sick, I could not get up out of bed and dress myself. Rick had to put some clothes on me and carry me to the car. Allison was extremely concerned. Rick persuaded her to get dressed and brought her to the neighbors who took her to school. She must have been so frightened to see me that way. We arrived at the emergency room and Rick had to carry me in. I can't begin to tell you how awful I felt. I thought for sure the leukemia was back and God was calling to me with a one-way ticket. He had given me three good years and I guessed that it was time to check out. I wanted to go quick and thought "no more chemo, no more suffering, just take me now." Rick carried me to a room. The attendant drew my blood to determine the cause. It was sent to the lab at once. I was instructed to urinate in a cup. Rick had to hold me on the toilet to get the specimen. I could not do anything on my own. He then took me back to my room. My oncologist came running down the hall to analyze the situation. When the blood tests came back the counts were great.

I was not going anywhere yet. I just had some sort of bug that required pumping some heavy antibiotics into me. I was told that I would need to stay in the hospital for a few days. I really didn't care at that point and only wanted to sleep. I could hardly remember the trip up to my room. By the afternoon in my hospital room, my temperature had risen to 105.0 degrees. I was delirious. I didn't even attempt to get out of bed to go to the bathroom. It was so horrible. The only reassurance I got was when a nurse entered my room and told me it would be all over by nightfall. It was learned that I had a common bacteria infection type pneumonia and that it would be gone within 24 hours. The nurse was right. By night, my temperature was normal and the only thing I had was a very bad headache and my heart hurt. I was glad the girls from the Phantom Regiment bugle corps were already gone on tour.

The next day, I felt great and was ready to go home, but the doctors at the hospital wanted to keep me for another day. I was bored and asked the nurse if there was anyone on the floor that I could talk to. She said there was a girl down the hall that also had leukemia that might be interested. I told the nurse to ask her if she would like to come see me in my room to talk. Within one-half hour, she was standing at my doorway.

The girl had just found out that she needed a bone marrow transplant and wanted to discuss details. I invited her in and explained the procedure. She was a few years younger than I. She had two siblings that were being tested as donors and she was waiting for the results. She was married and had a five-year-old daughter. We instantly got along and talked for hours about the leukemia process. I felt God had planted me in this hospital at this particular time to help her get through this. The following morning, I heard her coming down the hall with excitement. She had a match! We both hugged. I was so happy for her. That night her mother came to visit and I talked with both of them about the process and what to expect.

Support and love from family and friends are your greatest asset. I gave them, I hope, some good advice, wished her luck and told her that I would keep in contact. As I was preparing for bed, I felt a surge of energy throughout my body. It felt so good to help someone in need. It was such a wonderful feeling. "Maybe this is my calling," I thought.

The hospital discharged me the next morning. By 4:00 p.m., I was on my way to my hometown, a six-hour drive. Rick said I shouldn't go, just getting out of the hospital, but I easily persuaded him into it. Brian did the driving with Ally and me as passengers. While in the car, I felt a new sense of joyful energy in my system. It was so powerful that I thought I was going to burst. It was such a wonderful feeling. I had no aches and pains. I actually felt like a normal human being.

We celebrated my mother's 80th birthday with relatives and friends I had not seen for awhile. Going home is always a warm and loving experience. It is so simple and never overbearing.

In July I went to Madison for a checkup and the annual bone marrow biopsy test. The results indicated I was two years post transplant leukemia free. I realized I would be turning forty years old in a week. I could hardly believe I actually had made it. Ally was spending a couple of weeks with Grandma and Grandpa. It felt so strange without her. My stepson and his girlfriend came down to spend some time with us. I took them into Chicago for the day. We went to the museums, Sears tower, Navy Pier and Planet Hollywood. I was exhausted by the end of the day and didn't think I would make it. But once I started, I forgot the pain.

Well, the big day came. I was forty years old and still alive. What a great feeling! It felt so good to be here. Thank God for a second chance. I got all dressed up to go out to dinner with Rick and friends. To my complete amazement, Rick surprised me with a birthday party at a local club. When I walked in, there were all my friends. Some I had not seen for a long time. It was the first surprise party I had ever had. Rick even hired a caricature artist to draw everyone's portrait. Life is good!

In August, Ally and I took a two-week vacation visiting friends and relatives. I started out by driving to Eau Claire to visit my close friend Mary, and spend the night. Then we headed for Superior to spend some time with my sister and her family. We went sightseeing and shopping. We had an enjoyable time coming home to her house, especially relaxing in her Jacuzzi.

Next, we went to my mom's house for a couple of days. By the time I got to my mom's, my legs started to pulsate with pain. The rash on my skin had gotten worst and was flaring up again. I still tried to maintain my strength but was losing the battle. I was determined to go on. It was so hot and humid that the sweat was making my skin very itchy. I was truly miserable. I wondered how I was going to get through the rest of the vacation.

When I think back on my visits during this vacation, I remember the way my lovely mother tried to comfort me in any way she could to ease the pain. My sister was always trying so hard to find a cure for my pain and misery. God bless them both for their efforts. For the first time I really realized how dedicated my brother was to his community. I was seeing him in a whole new light. He has dedicated his life to helping others. He is always on the go, busy building this and that for everyone. He is a dedicated teacher and coach to the high school. He always finds time to come see me when I am visiting at my mother's house. There was softball tournament for girls in town and he umpired the games. His wife also told me he helped build the little league field in his spare time. I have great admiration for him.

When I started to feel a little bit better I went on my next adventure to Michigan and picked up my stepdaughter, Nikki. We traveled to Bayfield to hop the ferry to Madeline Island. We spent a few days with my sister and her family again at their cabin, a lovely, peaceful place. Across the street, is their sandy beach on Lake Superior from where it seems the shoreline can be seen forever. It always feels so peaceful, quiet, and lovely out there. Every night we had a bonfire, roasted marshmallows and s'mores and sang campfire songs while my sister's husband, Doug, played the guitar. He is one of the nicest men I know. The kids were even daring enough to go swimming in Lake Superior. I even got brave and went swimming. It was very cold at first, but after awhile I couldn't even feel how cold it was and it felt good on my skin.

The next day it was time to go. We hopped back on the ferry and headed back to my mom's house for the day. The following day, I dropped Nikki off at her hometown and drove to my last stop in Green

Bay to visit my in-laws. I was so exhausted by the time I got there that I just went to bed.

The next morning, before I left for home, I gave my mother-in-law an angel stamp for the letters and cards she writes. She is really into angels. I had bought her one months ago but couldn't find it, so I had to buy her another one just before I left. (Little did I know the significance of that lost angel.) I also took Rick's brother's kids and his sister's girl back home with me for a week. I thought it would be great for all of us to get to know everyone a little bit better since we only see each other for the holidays. It would be good for Rick, too.

It was great being home again. However, the temperature was very hot and muggy and we didn't have air conditioning. My house would get so hot that I would be literally soaked with sweat. The sweat dripped on my skin, which made it unbearably itchy. I had to take three showers a day to cool off to feel better. The kids were not used to this hot weather, either. It was uncomfortable for everyone. Everyday I tried to take them somewhere that was air-conditioned. When the week was over, I drove halfway and met Rick's sister to drop the kids off.

In late September my rash started to get worse. I was raw under my arms and around my waist. I could not even touch those areas because it was so painful. I had to take painkillers every day to relieve the aching. Every night I took an oatmeal bath to help stop the itch. I decided to increase the Prednisone by 5mg; my doctor said it might help the itching.

Then my big toe started to hurt. I could no longer get into our waterbed, so the couch had to do. My skin was getting tighter and tighter and it was getting very difficult to even move. By the end of the week, I could no longer get into my tub. My legs would no longer bend. Rick had to go out and buy me a cane.

In order to sit on my sofa, I would just fall onto it. Then, once I was down, I could not get up unless someone would help me. I could only wear moo-moo type dresses and could no longer reach to put on my socks. If there was nobody around to help, I had to go without. I could no longer wear any of my underwear, only Rick's seemed to be comfortable. I would use moisture therapy lotion every night to help relieve the extremely dry condition of my skin. It seemed that everyone I knew sent all kinds of lotions to help me. I had to forget wearing a bra, as it was impossible. It was so degrading to have to depend on others to help.

My big toe was so painful that I had to go to a foot doctor. He discovered I had an infection, which was the first of numerous ones from that time on. Would there be any end to the misery? I even had to find a "new way" to use toilet paper using my cane, since my hands were not able to stretch. (You figure it out.)

I was feeling very sorry for myself and decided to go to the support group again. I learned that two people in the group had already died since the last time I had attended a meeting. I thought, "At least I'm still here." When I first walked in using my cane, no one recognized me. They were shocked when they discovered it was me.

The next day, I felt pretty good. You cherish days like that, not knowing how long feeling good will last. It was a good day and it even seemed liked my skin symptoms had calmed down a little.

I went to Madison for a checkup and my doctor increased the Prednisone. He said I should get a physical therapist to help stretch my legs to help them from contractures. He also said I should take an exercise swim class. My skin felt like a piece of wood and was very itchy. I carried a back scratcher wherever I went. My back was constantly itchy. The doctor said it would eventually go away and to just hang in there. It was part of the GVHD of the skin. It had not attacked any of my internal organs, and I was thankful for that. It could have been worse.

But my right foot was giving me a lot of pain, especially at night. No matter where I moved it, it hurt. I learned that this is a condition called Restless Legs Syndrome, and that it would go away. "At least there will be an end to this misery," I thought. I felt like making a phone call to England to see if I could order one of those ancient torture machines where they string you up, pull a crank and stretch you. I would have loved to have one of those.

I woke up the next morning and felt just awful. I ached all over and my temperature rose to 103.0 degrees. Rick drove me to the emergency room. My chest just ached all over and my right lower back was in pain. By the time my name was called as I waited in the emergency room, my fever had broken and I had started to feel better. I decided to just go home. I did not want to spend any more time in the hospital.

I still didn't feel any better the next day. I called the doctor and requested to have a chest x-ray and blood work done. He agreed in order to make sure that I did not have any infections. I hoped that I did not have pneumonia, which would mean I would have to be hospitalized. I just could not do that to my family again. It seemed to me they had no life but to cater to me all the time and I could not take much more of that. I was really starting to get discouraged.

Then I got some good news. I only had an infection in my blood stream and could go to the doctor's office everyday day for intravenous antibiotics for a week, instead of going into the hospital. I was relieved to hear that. My first appointment was agonizing. It took six nurses and twelve tries to put an IV in me (my Hickman tubes had been taken out after 100 days). My skin was so tough that they could not get through it. My arms anguished in pain. It took over an hour to get a needle through to a good vein, and finding a good vein continued to be difficult to do everyday for the entire week. The nurses and I were both delighted when the week was over.

The support group leader called and informed me they were having a Good Luck party for one of the leukemia patients I had talked to. She was having a transplant done in Madison soon and invited me to come. I really wanted to go, but I decided to stay away. I did not want her to see me in this condition. She had enough to worry about with the transplant, let alone to see what GVHD might do to her.

Chapter 10

Total Misery

*Through hardship you learn
and grow stronger.*

The GVHD spread and was all over my skin. My right leg was very stiff and sore, especially at night. Each ankle had several raw sores on each side. It was hard to turn my neck from side to side and my skin was very tight. I had blisters and crusty patches growing rapidly on both sides of my stomach, underneath my knees, upper thighs and under my arms. I was not having trouble writing, however, or even using my hands, although they seemed arthritic. I would get cramps in them all day off and on.

I was very bloated all over my body from the Prednisone. Despite my physical shape, my mind still told me I could do normal things. The day before had been a very frustrating day. I had tried to make a pot roast and dropped most of the potato peelings on the floor. I could not find the pan to put it in, and when I reached to look for it my underarms would hurt. Then my hands decided to go into the arthritic mode and I dropped flour all over the floor. The bad thing about it was that I could not bend down to pick anything up. I swore a lot to myself that day.

When you are in the condition I was in, you want so bad to get your house clean or to go grocery shopping or to even do laundry, but you can't because you do not have any energy. My legs felt like they weighed one hundred pounds each. All you want to do or can do is just lie in bed. It was so frustrating to me. I struggled with insomnia and could hardly sleep at night. I also was having a leakage problem. I could not seem to do any thing too physical or I would wet myself. After awhile this problem subsided.

Mary from Milwaukee called and wanted to take me to lunch. It took her awhile to convince me to get out of the house and go. She stopped by to pick me up and literally had to shove me into her vehicle and then pull me out. It would take a lot of energy for me to get up from any-where. I had to hang on to something and pull myself up. As we were eating lunch, I realized I had to go to the bathroom. We were sitting by four men dressed in business suits. As I tried to pull myself up, I let out a "loud" one. Everyone stopped eating and looked shocked. I was so embarrassed that I didn't want to come out of the bathroom. I probably ruined everyone's lunch. We laughed at it later, but it sure wasn't funny at the time.

At one point, I started to investigate alternative medicine. I went to see an acupuncturist to see if he could help me. He was very considerate and knowledgeable. He took one look at my tongue and said my legs and hands were begging for blood supply. He said he could help me, but that my insurance company would not cover it. Too bad insurance does not recognize alternative medicine as a healing method. He told me to eat a lot of green leafy vegetables.

I went back home and rethought what I could do. My doctor had suggested using a physical therapist and doing water exercises. I decided to take his advice. I was still dropping things a lot and continued to use my massager to help the itching. I was still not able to put my socks on without great difficulty. Tying shoes was impossible. My posture was horrible. My stomach stuck out, while my back curved in and I could not straighten my legs. Bending at the knees was impossible.

My husband even tried to put lotion all over me and wrap me in saran wrap. He got the idea from wrapping the Thanksgiving turkey to keep it moist. (Thank God he got one of those already-made Thanksgiving dinners from the grocery store. There was no way I could have cooked that year.) The next day I woke up feeling better. My skin seemed to be stabilizing. I hoped it was burning itself out. I thought to myself, "It sure would be nice." Normal was only a word to me.

Eventually I took my doctor's advice and I went to physical therapy. For the first time, I actually wore sweats. It really felt good just to get out of the house and talk to someone else other than my family. A friend suggested I should see a massage therapist to help circulate my blood flow. Since I was very sensitive about my body's appearance, I wanted to find someone who would not be shocked by my appearance. I called around and found a nurse who did therapeutic massage to help cancer patients. She understood my problem and gave wonderful massages that made my skin feel better. We both agreed that traditional and alternative medicine should go hand in hand. I wish the doctors and the insurance companies would recognize how important this would be to patients. I firmly believe that with a combination of the two, a person would get better quicker and probably stay healthy.

I also started to go to an arthritis swim class at the YMCA. The instructors that ran the program were very sincere and really made me feel at ease. We stayed in the water about forty-five minutes and did a lot of stretching exercises. My legs felt so good afterward. There were quite a few of us, and I had a wonderful time with them. We even exchanged recipes.

It was time for another checkup in Madison and my doctor put me on Cyclosporine for my skin. Cyclosporine is extremely toxic to the kidneys. I hated taking all these different kinds of drugs. This particular medicine was very expensive. I called the Leukemia Society to see if they would help me pay for it. I had a list of drugs that they would help pay for, and this one was actually on the list. When I called, though, they told me that this specific drug was in a pilot program and no funds were available. I could not believe it, since Cyclosporine is a common bone marrow drug used to help stop GVHD. Needless to say, I was disappointed.

I had to sleep with my shoes on one night. Ally was sick and I couldn't ask her to help me with them. Rick could not help because he was out of town hunting. I finally had to give up trying to take them off. I almost called my neighbor to come over, but I chickened out. Oh well, it wasn't all that bad and I didn't have to struggle to put them on the next day.

Physical and massage therapy along with swimming helped to relieve some of the pain. It was the only time I seemed to be able to get out of the house at the time. I actually took a real hard look at my body in the mirror. It was so ugly; I looked like an alien. I could be ET's mother. I was growing peach fuzz on my face and had to shave once in awhile. It was so hard to feel feminine. For some reason I had shorts on when Rick came home from his trip. He could not believe it when he looked behind my knees and actually saw holes in my skin. My skin had ripped and you could see the flesh. I had one big hole underneath each knee. I never knew this because I could not see back there. I got a mirror and took a look. It was real nasty. Now I knew why I was in so much pain. I felt so embarrassed and self-conscience about myself. I must have looked awful to everyone. I started to get short with my family. It was so hard to be nice when I felt so miserable.

My husband and I got into a quarrel and I stormed out the door. I got into my Mustang and took off. I drove and drove with tears streaming down my face. I could hardly see the road. I ended up in the mall parking lot. I got out and mustered up all the energy I had to walk inside the mall. I sat on the first bench I could find. I was covered with sweat and my legs barely made it. I just sat there and watched the people go by.

There were couples and children with their parents laughing, carrying Christmas packages. Everyone seemed to be having such a good time. I wanted so much to be like those people. I wanted so much to be normal. I wanted to stay there forever and just watch.

What was I doing? Now I had my family mad at me. But I didn't care. I did not want to go home. I just wanted to sit there and watch people, happy people. It felt so good to get out and see different scenery. I stayed there until the mall closed. Finally, I had to go home. I walked into the house. We didn't speak to each other at all that night. I just did not care anymore. I was starting not to care about anything. I stopped cleaning or doing anything around the house. I had always been such a strong person. Now I was beginning to fall apart. I did not know how much more I could take. I did not understand why God was putting me through it all. Or was I putting myself through it? I wondered what had happened to my positive attitude. Then it occurred to me, "Ask and you shall receive." So it says in the Bible.

Well, I started to beg. I was at rock bottom and had nowhere else to go but up. I thought, "Please let me get on with my life." I felt that I could not handle anymore suffering. I prayed, meditated, and then just fell asleep. That night I awoke and felt a warm sensation on my cheek. At first I panicked and thought I had a temperature again. I took my temperature and it was normal. I realized my whole body seemed to experiencing an inviting warm sensation. This feeling lasted for three days. My skin seemed to be healing, and my self-esteem came back. I felt so much better and at peace with myself. Then I remembered my previous desperation. Had my prayers been answered? Was this a miracle? Why is it so hard to believe in miracles? Was it that simple, that all I had to do was pray and ask for help?

The next night, my daughter slept over at a friend's house. Since I could not get into the waterbed yet, I made up the sofa sleeper so my husband and I could sleep together for the night. We made up and I hugged him all night. The next day, I decided to change my daily activities around so it wouldn't be so boring. My mother called and told me about Vitamin E. I bought some and squeezed the liquid out onto my skin. I brushed it on with a brush. The result was that my skin was not as red anymore. I was willing to try anything.

Two weeks before Christmas I actually started getting excited about the holidays coming. My daughter put all the Christmas decorations up in the house while I supervised. With my doctor's approval, Rick had gotten me a handicapped card, so that I could go out and Christmas shop. I really didn't want to use it. I always felt too proud to do anything like that. But I realized that I needed help and had to learn to accept it, if only on a temporary basis. I gained a new profound admiration for handicapped people. I knew my handicap was temporary, but they had to deal with this everyday of their lives.

I started having real bad headaches. One night Rick had to wake me up twice because I was having nightmares. Maybe it was the whole box of chocolates I had eaten that night.

I went to Madison for another checkup for the first time since I had started to take Cyclosporine. The doctor found that my blood pressure was high and I was given a prescription for another pill for that. He also upped my Cyclosporine and Prednisone. I asked if everyone gets this skin GVHD, and he said that everyone's reaction is different. Some patients don't get any GVHD and go on to live normal lives. It figures that I would be one of those who would get it the worst. I also informed him of my recent weaknesses. He told me it is called myasthenia gravis. It is a neurological disorder characterized by extreme muscle weakness. I told him I had been feeling pretty good lately. I knew I had a lot to work on, but I felt a good change.

I had been keeping in contact with other leukemia patients and they were at one of the support group meetings I attended. It was nice to see everyone again. The next day, however, I started to feel real tired. I decided to try and take a nice warm shower. In the shower, I acciden-tally bumped into the hot water knob and the water was coming out scorching hot. I felt it burning on my skin. I finally managed to get out by knocking over the curtain and falling on the floor, desperately trying to get out. It was a very frightening experience. No one was home at the time.

My chest started to hurt and felt heavy. Sometimes when I slept, I could not catch my breath. My lower back throbbed at night and I had to continue taking painkillers to sleep. I also noticed what looked like an infection in my right eye. It was all bloodshot and red.

Ally and I went shopping and I was very exhausted and sweaty when we got home. I took my blood pressure, and the reading indicated it was a little high. I had never had high blood pressure till now. I accidentally dropped a couple of my pill bottles on the floor and hundreds of them spilled out. I had to put them all back in the right bottles. My eyes were going buggy, trying to get the right pills in the right bottles.

All night my right foot was in pain. It felt like someone was taking a knife and stabbing me with it. It was really excruciating. I finally took a painkiller. It still hurt, but the pain was reduced to what felt like a pin-prick. By the next day, I literally had a hole in my foot. It was wide open and I could see my flesh. It was awful. By now I knew that I had to be very careful about infections.

Rick and I were planning to go to Jamaica on vacation with other friends in May. I desperately wanted to go and enjoy myself, but I didn't know if would ever happen.

Linda, one of the ladies from our support group, called and wanted me to trace my hand on a piece of paper and send it to her. She was making a quilt for our support group leader and was placing each of our hands in each square. It turned out beautifully, and Angie still has it today.

Chapter 11

Strange Encounters of the Third Kind

> *Reality is only what we*
> *perceive it to be.*

For three months, strange psychotic behavior engulfed me from the medications that I was on. At the time, I was not aware of what was going on and neither was my family. The behavior initiated when I started to feel paranoid. I had a very short fuse and blew up at any little thing. I got confused over the smallest things. I felt like I had three separate minds. Paranoia dwelled in one mind, total frustration and belligerence dominated another mind, and a third mind was my normal self.

I started to think people were following me from the office, from my child's school, grocery shopping and so forth. I even had Rick follow me home one day because I was sure that people were following me. I also started to become very belligerent toward my husband. I don't know why I picked on him, but suddenly I felt as if he were my enemy. He tried to calm me down and even called the doctor and told him I was acting strange. I finally called the doctor myself and told him I was having terrible mood swings, and needed something to calm me down. He said he was so sorry I was feeling that way and prescribed Alprazolam to calm my nerves. I felt like a pill factory, and then I started having nightmares again. The only good news at this time was that Nikki had her baby. I was now a grandma to a beautiful little baby girl. All I could do was smile. Unfortunately, I was so out of it that I couldn't even get excited about it.

I would wake up every day very drowsy and crabby. I was not myself for about a couple of hours. I did my best to keep the frustration and anxiety from lashing out. It seemed like so much was going on in my mind, and I could not keep it straight. I knew I was not going crazy, but in my mind I kept hearing voices which are difficult to explain. I kept getting a fast, continuous rush of ideas, which made it difficult for me to sleep or think of anything else. It was all so very strange. I wanted to just mellow out and thought I should be happy and excited about the baby, but could not feel happy and excited because of the other feelings that had taken over my body. My right hand was also very bad and I could not use it much because it felt so clumsy and had no strength in it.

I felt like I needed to see my doctor, so Rick took me to Madison for a checkup. My blood pressure was very high and the doctor prescribed a different pill to lower it. He also lowered the Cyclosporine and was worried that I had a too high content of drugs in my blood. I was not surprised.

One weekend we traveled to Northern Michigan to see our first granddaughter. I wanted so desperately to go, no matter how hard it was for me. I endured pain most of the way up. I tried not to think about it. We finally reached our destination, four and one-half hours later. After fighting with ice and snow and with Rick on one side of me and the cane on the other, we finally entered the house. I sat down, got myself situated and Nikki put Taylor in my arms. The pain and the frustration were gone immediately. Holding this precious bundle, this beautiful gift of life, took my pain away.

I looked at all the features, the funny faces, the little quivers and the famous wide-mouthed yawns. They took my breath away. It was pure heaven and a moment and feeling that I will never forget. It was a miracle. That night Nikki, Chris, his girlfriend, Rick, Ally and I all went out to dinner. It felt good to see everyone again. I thought, "Too bad Brian couldn't be here to make our family complete."

The next day on the way home, I misplaced my painkillers. I was in so much pain in the car that I thought I was going to pass out. I had an unopened can of pop in my hand and would squeeze it hard to try and release some of the pain. I did not want to let anyone know and spoil any thoughts of a special visit. Of course, I finally found my medicine when we pulled into our driveway.

That night I did my visualization again. I did the vase thing and saw the figure again in black. This time I saw the face as she pulled off her hood. It was a beautiful lady with red wavy hair and I immediately felt a sense of ecstasy in her presence. She was magically beautiful. She sat down unto the ground as I walked over to her. I lay my head on her lap and she stroked my hair to comfort me. I felt at peace.

The next day, my mother called to inform me her brother had died and that she would be going to the funeral in Kenosha, which is about one hour from me. I told her I might as well go since I was so close. I was glad that I had taken her to see him that summer when she was here. She at least got to see him before he died. I revealed to her that I was now walking with a cane. She had not seen me in about a year and I wanted to prepare her for my appearance.

Brian, Ally and I drove to Kenosha. I thought it was important that the kids went. Rick stayed behind to run the office. We got there with no trouble, but arrived a little late. We just sat in the back of the church. My mother spotted us after Mass and we drove together to the restaurant where lunch would be served.

My mother was stunned. She could not get over the way I looked. I reassured her that it was just temporary and I would get my own body back again. My relatives hardly recognized me. I must have looked dreadful to them. But somehow I felt so much energy just being there with everyone. I thanked God for my children. Brian always came through for me. In my time of need, he was such a wonderful son and Ally was my little nurse. She would always step in to take care of me. We all had a nice time, even though it was a funeral. We said our good bye's and headed back home.

That night something strange happened. I was still sleeping on the couch because I still could not get in the waterbed. We had a lamp that was my maternal grandmother's by the piano across where I was sleeping. Grandmother had it in her house as far back as I can remember. It was in the middle of the night, about 12:45, and I noticed with my eyes shut that it seemed brighter in the room. I knew everyone was in bed and I didn't hear any footsteps. I finally had enough courage to open my eyes and saw that the lamp was on. It had just turned on all by itself. I got up and looked around the house to make sure everyone was in bed sleeping, and they were. So I went to shut it off. I lay back on the couch and just as I was starting to go to sleep, it went on again. I threw the covers over my head and thought, "I'm not getting up this time." Were my eyes playing tricks on me? I did not want to know. Early the next morning, I heard Rick get up and he turned off the lamp. It had been on all night.

I watched a TV show about brain tumors that featured Burzinski Clinic. I immediately called Kuster, who was our landlord at our office and had a business of his own next to ours. He was such a dear man. He had recently learned that he had cancerous brain tumors. Rick and I became friends to him and his family. Over the last couple of years he had lost his mother, sister, and other relatives from cancer. The doctors had told him that he did not have much time to live. He immediately quit work to be with his family. I told him not to give up. When I called, his daughter answered the phone and I told her to turn on the TV. Maybe this would give him hope and inspiration. I wanted so desperately to help him. He died a few months later.

In March I decided to take some pictures of exactly how my skin looked. I wanted something to remind myself of how lucky I was when I finally got better. By the next day I started to feel better. My skin symptoms had died down and it did not itch anymore. Pain and agony was no longer a part of me. I felt free.

My daughter and I went to a store so she could buy a CD. I noticed, as I got out of my car, there was a very handicapped man shuffling sideways in front of the store. He was very short and had on ragged clothes and boots. As I was approaching the store with my cane, I noticed I was going to run right into him. Everyone around was whispering and pointing at him. I went up to him and asked if he needed any help. He slowly turned his head and looked up and down at me and said, "You look like the one who needs help. I'm only going to the end of this block." He pointed to the end of the building with ripped gloves on and shuffled on. It was so strange. I thought about him the whole time we were in the store. We left the store only fifteen minutes later. We got into the car and I told my daughter we had to find him to see if he was all right. I drove around the block, behind the store, and up and down the street. He was no where to be found. He had vanished. We were both so puzzled.

For the next couple of days, I felt a sense of internal energy and informed Rick that I wanted go to Jamaica after all. I knew my physical body needed work and decided I would work hard at physical therapy. I had two months to work out before we would leave for Jamaica.

The day after I decided I would go to Jamaica, I had to go into the office to help Rick, since Brian was on vacation. It was a busy day and I was extremely exhausted when I got home and collapsed on the loveseat. Ally was sleeping over at someone's house and Rick had settled in watching TV on the couch. I tried to fall asleep, but I couldn't. Ideas kept flooding into my mind just like they had before, and my racing mind would not leave me alone. I tried to tell myself that these thoughts could not keep up continuously. I needed sleep and wanted the thoughts to stop, but they kept on and kept me awake. It was as though many different voices were whispering in my head all at the same time.

The next few paragraphs and as well as the following chapter were very difficult for me to write. There are a lot of embarrassing moments, but I wanted to tell it the way I had experienced it. At first I was just going to skip the whole thing, but I wanted to be as truthful as possible and my family and friends said it should be told. So here goes.

My daughter had a piano recital and I wanted to get her something special. I decided on a charm bracelet. I remembered a new jeweler that had just opened up in town and picked up the phone book to see if they were listed. Then all of a sudden, clear as day, a picture entered my mind of a comedian that had just recently passed away. In the image in my mind the comedian puffed on his cigar, blew it out, and said, "Hi, Kid." I wasn't afraid and welcomed him into my mind. He said, "The listing isn't in the phone book, so don't bother looking." I smiled and accepted what was happening to me. He told me that I was his first assignment and since he knew what the human body needed, he was going to take over the overwhelming thought processes in my head and slow them down a little. I felt instant relief.

Suddenly, the phone rang. It was Rick. He needed me to come into the office as soon as possible to help out. I hung up. Then the voice said, "We'll talk in the car." The traffic was insane and Ally was with me and was making conversation so it was hard to concentrate What I remember of "what he told me" is that I should get two movies he had made and watch them and that I could learn something from them.

We finally got to the office and I had to run back out to the bank and then stop to get lunch. I got back to the office and helped out for awhile. Just before we left, I blurted out my head conversation with the comedian to Rick. He had this real worried look on his face and I realized it was a bad idea to tell him about the "conversation." Immediately, I changed the subject.

I took Ally to my girlfriend's house so I could go shopping for the bracelet. The voice was with me all the way. After much running and coming around empty-handed, he finally told me where to go and I would find what I was looking for. He was right. I walked in, saw the perfect bracelet and a treble clef charm to match and asked to have them wrapped.

Then I went to the video store. To my surprise they didn't have any of the movies the comedian had made. I was dumbfounded. I went home and started calling all the video stores. None had the movies. I was totally confused. Then an image of him appeared, and he said to buy them. I hadn't thought of buying them. I phoned a video store and was put on ignore. He assured me that they would be there, so I hung up and jumped in the car. The traffic was nuts with cars everywhere. It seemed like the whole town was on the road. I finally get there and saw that all the handicapped parking spots were taken. Just as I was ready to swear in frustration, a vacant one became empty right in the very first row. I got a cart and entered the store. I looked and looked and was told I was looking in the wrong aisle, that the movies were in the next aisle. I searched and kept searching and could not find them. An employee was standing in front of me and I asked her where these movies were. She gently pushed me aside and pulled out the two movies. I had been looking in the wrong place. I thought this was too incredible. No one would believe this. Ally and I watched both videos that night. I did not want to push it on Rick.

For the first time in a long time, I had a peaceful night's sleep. I got up and got ready for the recital. Rick could not make brunch before the recital so I took my neighbor lady instead. She had retired a while ago and at one time had been a piano teacher with a very distinguished background. She also had played a number of other instruments and really liked Allison so I knew she would enjoy going. She talked a lot all the way to the recital and throughout brunch.

Ally wanted to go to the dessert table by herself to get something. I let her go and my neighbor all of a sudden stopped talking. She looked at me and said, "Well?" I said, "Well what?" She said, "Have you seen a miracle yet?" I said "Why?" and she told me that is about the only thing she hadn't seen yet in her lifetime and figured it had to be me. I didn't even hesitate and said, "Yes." She said, "I thought so." At that time my daughter came back and our neighbor lady guest continued on talking again as if nothing else had been said. It was never discussed between us again and I'm really not sure what she really meant by it.

The next day I had a hair appointment. As I was sitting under the dryer, the hairdresser handed me a magazine. My comedian was on the cover. I turned to the page where he was and almost burst out laughing. There he was exactly as he had first appeared to me. When I got home Rick called me. He said that the liquor store directly across from our business had just put up a cardboard likeness of my comedian holding a martini in the window and he was staring right at him. I could not believe it. I had to go up and look for myself. Sure enough, there he was. "This is too much," I thought. I had to go home and call my sister. When I arrived at home, I remember cleaning my stove with a rag, when all of a sudden, there in my mind, was my father. He smiled at me with tears in his eyes. My comedian was standing behind him, saying it was hard to get him to come, but finally with some coaxing he came. I broke down and sobbed uncontrollably. It was such an emotional feeling that it is impossible to describe.

I decided to call my sister. I had been telling her all that had been happening to me. I also told my classmate, Mary. She was jealous. There are too many coincidences that I can't ignore. My sister asked me if my father was wearing his glasses or not. I know it sounds strange, but I really couldn't answer that, nor could I tell you what he was wearing. It was a vision that was not quite human, but more emotional and spiritual. I also discussed it with Rick. He started to get frustrated with me. He believed it was all nonsense and I should immediately stop it all. He was furious. I was ordered to stop all voices and forget about what he thought was insanity. He did not want the subject to ever come up again. I felt so let down. How could I stop it when I was not in control?

We had been working hard in physical therapy to get my body in shape for Jamaica, although it had not cooperated very well. My skin felt a great stretch right after therapy, but tended to snap back in place by the next day. I compared it to a rubber band.

I decided it was about time to go shopping for an answering machine. Before we left for Jamaica, we needed to install one to answer calls while we were away. I was going to put my own message on it when an idea crossed my mind. I remembered I had bought an answering machine cassette a few years ago on clearance. The tape had impersonations of several well-known comics. I found it buried in the video cabinet. I placed it in the cassette deck and listened to them to decide which one I wanted to use. Suddenly, my comedian came on with a phone message. I was stunned. I laughed at the message he had given and couldn't help but use it. I thought about what Rick had said and went against his wishes.

That same day, I was looking for something in my china cabinet and found the angel stamp that I was going to give to my mother-in-law. I looked at it closely and it looked just like the lady in my visualization. She was a beautiful angel. Could this be my actual guardian angel? Could this be happening to me? We all have guardian angels, but to actually see mine? I was overwhelmed with an astounding, peaceful feeling. That night I did my visualization again. Immediately, I saw her. She gave me a big smile and grabbed my hand and pulled me into what seemed to be a meadow of flowers. She was so blissfully overjoyed. We held each other's hands and danced in circles in a beautiful meadow. She had on a dazzling violet dress that sparkled, and the sparkles seemed to illuminate all around her. I felt so much energy from her. I experienced her immense sense of freedom and happiness. Peacefully, I fell asleep.

I awoke in the middle of the night. My chest was in pain. I felt a heavy pressure and tried not to panic. Suddenly, I felt as though someone were doing surgery inside my chest. I lay very still and felt soothing warmth inside my chest. There was no pain. I fell into a deep, relaxed sleep. I awoke the next morning feeling better than I had in months.

Chapter 12

To Paradise and then Hell

Never underestimate
the power of the mind.

When we left for Jamaica, I had addressed seven letters to my daughter and had dated each one. I told her to open one up everyday to remind her of how much we loved her and were always thinking of her. We left for Jamaica via two other couples picking us up at 6:30 a.m. and took the bus to O'Hare. We got checked in and requested a wheel chair. It would have been difficult for me to walk all the way through O'Hare. The attendant wheeled me down right to the gate. That was good service. The plane left on time and the flight was fun. I kept coming up with jokes and everyone was laughing. They didn't know I could be so funny. Neither did I. I could never remember jokes before.

When we got off the plane, a wheel chair was waiting for me. I kind of liked this idea. Everyone else had to go through customs. I just had to sit and wait for everyone until they got their luggage. I was wheeled next to another lady in a wheel chair. She was with her daughter. Her mother seemed a little confused and could not find her passport. She started to pull everything out of her purse. The she started to argue with her daughter about not being able to find her passport, but would not give her daughter the purse. I was stuck in the middle of these two arguing and it was beginning to get on my nerves. So I grabbed the purse from the mother and handed it over to the daughter to take a look. She found it instantly.

Finally, I was wheeled right to the car and we were driven to the house. The house was privately owned by a doctor who rented it out discreetly when he was not there. It was a beautiful one-story house up on a hill. It had four bedrooms, each with its own separate bathroom and terrace. A big swimming pool overlooked the ocean. We had a cook, maid, and butler at our service.

We quickly unpacked and sat around the pool and relaxed until dinner was served on a dining room table out near the patio. The table setting was gorgeous and filled with flower petals all around. The dinner was exquisite and the dessert was heaven. After supper, we just sat around and enjoyed the view. The men decided to explore a little of the island, while the women stayed behind. It had been an exhausting day for me. My legs felt like they were on fire. I tried to live with it but gave in and took some painkillers and went to bed.

The next morning we all woke up and had a lovely breakfast. The fresh fruit was picked daily from the trees on the premises. The food and fresh fruit was spectacular. After breakfast, we decided to go to the nearest place so the guys could watch the Chicago Bulls game. The girls sat together and had some nice conversations. Later, we all went back to the house to a lovely meal and then went to bed early. The guys had made plans to go fishing the next day and the girls were going to go shopping with the cook.

Our first trip was to the meat market. The cook picked out a large piece of meat and asked if it would be okay for supper. We all looked at each other and shrugged our shoulders. We had no idea what it was and really didn't want to know. Next stop was the fresh fruit and vegetable market. Our driver and the cook's husband were also with us. We all piled out of the vehicle and the cook started to bicker over prices with the merchants. The sun was beating down on us and I decided to get out of the sun and find a place to sit in the shade. Well, the minute I found some shade, my two friends and the cook were right beside me. The cook explained that I should not be alone and could not leave her side. My friends explained to the cook that I could not be in the sun. She proceeded to find a merchant in the market located in the shade, so I could sit. Bless her heart. Her husband and the driver stayed very close to our sides. I looked around and realized we were the only Americans there. When we were done, we went to a grocery store. It was much like our corner "Ma and Pa" stores at home. On our last stop we shopped in a little mini-mall. My legs were killing me, but I used my mental ability to overcome the pain, and concentrated on shopping instead.

I tried to do my exercises in the pool every night. The water worked to cool my body exposed to the tropical heat. Most of the rest of the week I just stayed around the house and read. The last day there, we decided to go to another town across the island. It was a long and exhausting drive. Our friends decided to go snorkeling while Rick stayed with me. I started to feel pain all over and wondered if maybe I should not have come along for the drive. I thought maybe I had heat stroke and was dehydrated. I lay down in the back of the van all the way home. I felt better when we got back.

The next day, we traveled back to the States. We finally reached home by nightfall. I was just exhausted and literally fell into bed.

We woke up the next day and called Rick's mom so that we could talk to Allison. She missed us very much and could not wait to come home the next day. Brian planned to meet them in Madison to pick up Allison and bring her home. I couldn't wait to see her.

Something very bizarre happened to me the next morning. I started to hallucinate. I was not quite sure how or why it started. My mind started to play tricks on me. Brian was at the house getting ready to go pick up Allison. I had started to behave abnormal. He called Dad at the office, then jumped into the truck and left. The next thing I knew Rick was at the house. To this day I don't know why, but I turned belligerent on him. I started to throw my silver pieces on the floor and just started to scream at him. Right then, there was a knock on the door. When Rick went to answer it I sneaked out of the house, jumped in the car with no shoes on, and hurried off. I had decided that I was going to pick up Allison in Madison by myself. I'm not quite sure how I made it to the freeway since it was raining cats and dogs. I could hardly see until I got onto the freeway.

On the freeway, I came to the automatic tollbooth. I had no money and started to search the car for loose change. I looked up and saw numerous cars behind me. I thought to myself how angry I would have been if I had been one of them. I finally found the exact change and drove off. The rain turned into a downpour. Many cars were pulling over to the side. I, on the other hand, felt as if I was in God's hands, in a trance. Every time I could not see very well, lightning would flash right in front of me and I could see clearly down the road. I had no fear and felt like angels were all around protecting me.

I finally reached Madison and ended up on the top ramp of the UWM hospital and parked the car. I stayed in the vehicle and the paranoid feeling I had experienced before started to set in. I was not quite sure why I was there. I started to get confused about the whole thing. Then I saw a custodian coming up the ramp in a golf cart. He jumped out and started to hose down the ramp.

I stepped out of the car and proceeded toward him. I ask if he had any shoes or socks for me in the cart. He looked at me puzzled and said, "No." I began to get irritated with him and I think he realized I wasn't all there. I got mad at him and pulled a broom out of his cart and started to chase him down the ramp with it. The poor guy. He dropped the hose and ran, probably faster than he had ever run before in his life. I stopped chasing him and put the broom back into the cart. I figured that would fix him for not having shoes for me and sat back in my car.

It only took a few minutes and a man with a walkie-talkie came up by the car and said, "We found her." Next thing I knew, two squad cars had pulled up beside me. I wondered what this was all about. I suddenly locked the doors. I had it in my paranoid mind that they might try to harm me or take me somewhere where I could not be found.

Four police officers tried to get me out of my car. One was becoming very impatient with me. I don't know why, but I asked them if there was a rookie in the group. A nice young guy said he was and was very soft spoken. I felt like I could trust him. I agreed to come out if he took me to the hospital, and only to the hospital. He agreed. So, I opened the door and the one cop grabbed my hand and yanked me out of the car. I told him my legs hurt and I could not walk so well but he didn't seem to care. He practically threw me into the squad car. The nice cop drove me to the ER. He opened the door for me and helped me out of the car. I was very humble to him and thanked him for his patience and help.

When we got to the ER, I told a staff member to call my doctor in the hospital and he would explain who I was. I was put in a waiting room while the staff figured out what to do with me. I just sat there patiently waiting. Meanwhile, outside my door there were three different men with brown uniforms. One was laughing and said they should just send me to a funny farm, lock me up and throw away the key. I was so hurt by that comment. I was a living and loving human being. How could anyone make a sick joke out of this? They didn't even know anything about me. I knew I wasn't crazy. I knew something was wrong with me, but didn't know what.

My belligerent mind started to take over. In my cantankerous state, I was determined to get even. The individual who made the comment went to sit down in the waiting room which was right across the hall from me. I looked over to him and glared at him with a demonic eye. I just kept on staring. At first he could care less. But as I just kept on staring he got up and closed the door halfway. He was chewing gum, so I decided to walk across and ask nicely if he had any more gum. As I opened the door, he started to raise his voice at me to get back. He informed me it was diabetic gum and I couldn't have any.

As I started to walk back to my room, I heard him snicker. That did it. I became furious! I turned and started to shout that there is no such thing as diabetic gum and I'm not crazy and I'm not stupid! He finally tossed me a piece of gum that landed on the floor. My legs could not bend so I couldn't pick it up. A nurse came and asked what was going on. I explained the situation to her and I wanted him out of my sight. I told her I had never done anything to him and all I wanted was a little respect. So, I said my say and went back to my room. The phone rang in my room and I answered it in a pleasant manner. A sergeant introduced himself and asked to speak to the nice police officer. I went out into the hall and called for him. He hung up after the call and escorted the man out of the room across the hall. I never saw him again. A hospital attendant entered my room and explained the rooms on the psychiatric ward were full. I would have to be moved to another hospital. If my doctor agreed, I would go. I had complete faith in him for what was best for me at that time. He agreed only so they could monitor me to find out what was wrong with my mind. The nice policeman was waiting for me, and he drove me to the other hospital. I was grateful for his kindness.

I had never been in or near a place like this before in my life. At first it didn't matter because of the state I was in. I couldn't remember much about coming in that night. (I had a pretty busy day.) I woke up the next morning and realized where I was. I decided to get up and investigate the place. The floor was restrictive and small. The only door to the outside world was locked. A phone near the nurses' station was the only way to communicate with the outside world. The lounge was the only place television could be watched and meals could be eaten.

The first patient I caught sight of was a lady who just walked up and down the hall constantly, back and forth. The second patient I saw was an old guy who mumbled to himself and was always lying down on the sofa. Then there was a guy around my age who didn't seem all that bad. Breakfast, lunch, and dinner were served at a certain time and you had to be there or you would miss out. I tried to be the perfect patient, afraid to make any wrong moves. At the time I was not aware why I was there and was afraid to ask. So I tried to handle it as best as possible.

By the time lunch came around I had noticed my speech and train of thought were very slow. I felt like I was going in slow motion. I had a hard time concentrating on TV and decided to spend the rest of the day in my room. I ended up getting a roommate for the night, whom I had no desire to meet. She had a bizarre behavior about her. I am not sure what she was doing in bed, nor did I care so I just got up and went into the TV room until she fell asleep. I then went back into the room. I had a hard time sleeping, not knowing what this lady was capable of doing.

The next morning something very odd happened. The woman got up early and went across the hall, knocked on the door, and went in. She came back about 20 minutes later. I have to explain that the men are on one side of the hall and the women are on the other side. You figure it out. I was appalled but didn't dare say anything in fear of getting in trouble. Thank God, she left that day.

I got up and went to breakfast. I ended up sitting with the guy around my age. I'll call him "Lenny." I decided to introduce myself and he did the same. We were both on the same kind of drug, so we talked like robots. It was so hard to concentrate. For instance, when lunch came around, I said "Hi Lenny" and he said "Hi Fran." Then as he left he said, "Bye Fran," and I said, "Bye Lenny." End of conversation. By dinner, I could actually make a sentence. For some reason we talked about family. I told him my sister was from Superior. He said his mother was from Superior. The guy wasn't all that bad. He could at least make some normal conversation.

The old guy was yelling something about politics to himself. Then the lady started to pace up and down the hall again. She was really sobbing. I felt so sorry for her that I went out and put my arms around her and asked what was wrong. She said her only son got killed in a car accident and her mother and father also were killed in another car accident. No wonder why she was there. It must have been too much for her to take. The next day she introduced me to her only son who came up to visit her. Boy, was I gullible. She was way out there.

Later, in the TV room, the old guy was sleeping on the couch. Everyone there complained that he always watched political shows and wouldn't let anyone else touch the clicker. I was still in my somewhat belligerent state and grabbed the clicker. He woke up and demanded it back. I yelled at him to explain how he could watch TV and sleep at the same time. I informed him I was going to be in charge of the clicker from now on and he would have to answer to me. He had no complaints. I then gave the clicker to the other patients and advised them to watch what they wanted. If he gave them any trouble, I would take care of it.

The attendants were coming and going. I knew they were there to watch our activities. I tried to talk to them, but they seemed very unsociable. There was one attendant who came in who was very nice and treated me like a normal person. He was really interested in finding out about my comedian. Most of the others acted cold and distant. They usually wouldn't have a conversation with anyone. I saw the doctor every day for about an hour. I can't remember too much about the conversations we had.

I went to sit down for lunch and Lenny was across from me again. We did the "Hi" routine. He asked me where I was from. When I told him, he said he had an aunt that lived in the same place. End of conversation. At dinner, he sat down across from me again. We did our little dialogue and then he asked me where my brother lived. I gave him the name of the town and remarkably his brother also lived there. I started to realize Lenny wasn't all there, either.

Not being able to cope with the other patients, I spent the rest of the day in my room. In a way I felt so sorry for them. What could have possibly made these people so out of it? They were in their own little world. They had no idea what went on beyond that. How can people live like that? I really couldn't see that they were getting any help here, either. A doctor might talk to them for an hour, and then they were on their own. I guess we are all basically on our own. I'm no psychiatrist, but it seems to me that people like that need more attention as to what really lies beneath their misery.

I was especially feeling blue the next day. An attendant arrived to wheel me down to the physical therapist on another floor. As I was waiting in the waiting room, I looked up and saw a picture similar to the one my sister had given me for Christmas. The picture she gave me was of two sisters, dressed in Victorian clothes, having tea together. The picture on the wall was of the same two sisters, only they were walking side by side near a shore. It gave me so much comfort to see this. It felt like my sister was watching over me. I felt so much emotion that I began to cry silently in my wheel chair.

That night, I decided to call my classmate friend, Mary in Eau Claire. She started telling jokes and made me laugh. I told her I was thinking about acting out the Jack Nickelson episode in the movie, *One Flew Over the Cookoo's Nest*. I was going to turn off the TV and pretend there was a baseball game going on and that I would call the plays. This time I had her laughing on the floor. I decided against it since they would probably keep me there longer.

Rick and Ally came to visit. (Brian and Rick came right away when I had first arrived to bring me clothes. They didn't stay because I was still acting very belligerent.) I couldn't wait to see my daughter again. I wanted so desperately to go home with them. I begged them to take me out of this crazy place. I couldn't take much more of this. He refused, knowing how important it was for me to stay. I wouldn't listen. Rick convinced me to call my sister and ask her. He knew it was the only way

I would stay, if she said I should. I called her and she advised me to stay. I told her I wasn't crazy. She said she knew that. Then she asked me if I knew why I was there. I told her I didn't know. She explained to me that one of my medications had made me that way and it wasn't anything I did that was wrong. They had to slowly lower it to a safe level before I could leave so I wouldn't be that way anymore. They diagnosed me with drug-induced psychosis. I thanked her for telling me why and felt much better. So I decided it was best for me to stay. It must have been so hard on my daughter. I couldn't imagine the hell she was going through all over again. So they left without me. I went into my room and cried. My Madison doctor called and wanted to talk. I was too embarrassed to talk to anyone and refused.

In order to take a shower in the psychiatric hospital, you had to ask an attendant to unlock the door for you. The showers are situated at the end of the hall with two separate doors, one for each shower stall. I asked an attendant to open one for me. There was a small room before the entrance to the shower that had a bench to sit down on. I began to undress. As I was getting ready to stand up and go into the shower, the door opened up and there was Lenny standing there staring at me. The attendant closed the door. I was totally humiliated. Was it an honest mistake or a prank? I didn't want to know and kept it to myself.

Within a few days, I started to feel like my old self again. The voices in my head were all gone and my belligerent behavior ceased to exist. I was moved to the other side of the ward, where there was more freedom. At first, I was terrified of the unknown, but relieved once I got there. There were a lot more people in this ward and they could carry on a conversation. It felt so good to talk to someone normal. I don't know what I would have done if I had to stay in the other place any longer. I actually went to a craft class and made several things for Ally.

I was put in a group therapy session. We all got to take turns and talked about our problems. Most of the other patients' problems had started with bad childhood memories and escalated throughout their lives. They had no sense of direction when they were little and no role models to follow since their parents were out of it. When it was my turn to talk, I almost felt guilty telling them how wonderful my childhood was. They all stared at me in silence. I told them the only reason I was there was because of a high dose of a prescription drug I was taking. That was the last session I went to.

Rick's mom and dad came to visit and two of my friends also came the same day. I was embarrassed to see them. They immediately made me feel comfortable. They knew that it wasn't anything that I did that caused my psychosis. It felt really good to have contact with really normal people. I don't know how people found the strength to work at the hospital. After my company left, one of the nurses asked if I wanted to go down to the chapel and go to the service. I thought it might be a good idea. As I was listening to the service, I noticed a prayer etched in glass on the window. It was beautiful. It went something like this:

> *Make me an instrument of peace,*
> *where there is hatred, let me sow love,*
> *where there is injury, pardon,*
> *where there is doubt, faith*
> *where there is despair, hope*
> *where there is darkness, light*
> *and where there is sadness, joy*
> *Grant that I may not so much seek to be consoled, as to console*
> *to be understood, as to understand, to be loved, as to love*
> *for it is giving that we receive,*
> *it is pardoning that we are pardoned,*
> *and it is in dying that we are born to eternal life.*

That just about says it all. I asked the minister where the prayer came from. He said it was a prayer of Saint Francis of Assisi. I should have known. I felt like it was meant for me. (They just spelled "Frances" wrong) When I got back up to my room, they informed me I was going home the next day.

Chapter 13

Deep Depression and Frustration Set In

Friendship...never explain.
Your real friends will accept you
no matter what you believe in.

Rick arrived early to take me home. I couldn't wait to get out and put the incident of the psychiatric hospital in my past. It was such an ordeal for everyone. I was amazed at how I was able to handle all of it.

My daughter came home from school and we both gave each other a big hug. I could see the excitement on her face. She said she had missed me so much and thought that I would never be able to come home to see her again. I explained to her what had happened and why I had to stay there for awhile. She has had such a strange childhood. I hope in some odd way, it will make her stronger in her life. I will make it up to her someday.

I called Brian and apologized for what I had put him through. I was embarrassed, but as always, he understood. We have always had a special bond. Rick was upset with my doctor for not letting us know about the potential drug side effects. I, on the other hand, was not. It was hard for my doctor to keep track of me when I lived so far away from where he practiced.

My friends almost immediately came over to see how I was doing. I still had a hard time talking to them with the drug, Haloperidol, in my system. I called my doctor and he agreed with my request to terminate using the drug. The drug's effect took a few days to wear off. The mood-swing drug that put me in the hospital in the first place was the steroid drug, Prednisone. I now know to never take this steroid in high doses again. I wanted to get off it completely. I also looked like I had lost twenty pounds.

The next day, Ally came home and presented to me a potted plant. She was glad that I felt better from my cancer. It was the first time she had ever used the word "Cancer" to describe my illness. She somehow felt it was safe to say it.

That summer we opened our pool and had many friends over. They were all so dedicated to me in all that I had been through. I learned they were all at the house with Rick the day I took off. They were all trying to find me. They even drove around looking for me. My friend called the police and explained to them what had happened. Rick called my doctor in Madison and advised him of the situation. They immediately called the Wisconsin State police to search for me. I had two states looking for me. I felt so embarrassed about it, but they reassured me not to be. I felt so much comfort in their friendship. We were really puzzled when Rick asked how I ever got to Madison that day without stopping for gas. He explained that the gas tank had been on empty when he got home that day and I couldn't have made it to Madison on what was in the tank. I didn't have any money so I couldn't have stopped for gas. I must have been driving on fumes. (I like to think that maybe an angel was lending its wings.)

The next day, Ally and I decided to go to the animal shelter and pick out a kitty. (I talked to my doctor to make sure it was OK.) She was so excited. As we looked at the last cage, there was a little kitty that had come right up to her. I could see them both bonding. She had no doubt. She wanted that one. So we took it home. She was one happy little girl. It felt so good to see her smile again.

I began to realize how much my husband had to endure throughout this whole process. He continued to be stressed out. He was trying to juggle a lot of balls in the air. I wished that I could do something for him. I knew he didn't mean anything by it, but he said he wished someone would come up to him and ask how he was doing for a change instead of asking how I was doing. I really felt sorry for him. I knew he was getting tired of all this. We finally started talking about what happened to me on the Prednisone. We really hadn't discussed it with each other. It was too embarrassing for both of us and hard to believe all that had happened. He told me Ally had run out of the hospital into the parking ramp hysterically crying the day I demanded them to take me home. It took him almost an hour to find her. She was hiding in a corner of the ramp. He finally got her into the car and she did not speak to him all the way home. We talked for hours about the whole ordeal. We cried and ended up laughing about the incident. What else can you do? I keep thinking of that poor man I chased with the broom. I hope I will be able to tell him I'm sorry someday. I would also like to thank the nice young police officer.

It had been three years since I had my transplant. My girlfriend called me one day and said I needed a night out. The group "The Monkees" were coming to town and insisted she and I and some other friends of ours should go to the concert. I agreed. We even bought 70's clothes to wear. It sure brought back some great memories. It was just what the doctor ordered.

The day after the concert I decided to go into the pool by myself to do some exercises. I needed to strengthen my legs. I lost my footing and began to go under. Fear and panic engulfed me. I realized I could drown. After all that I had been through, I wouldn't allow this to happen. I just found the strength within me and managed to get to the side of the pool and pull myself out. I never swam alone again.

I had not been to a support group in awhile, and decided to attend. Most of the people who had been in my first support group had either died or gone on with their lives. I told everyone at the meeting about my whole ordeal. It felt good to get it out of my system. The entire group gave me wonderful moral support. They were all such a brave group. I always left the meetings feeling energized by their inspiration.

I had numerous toe infections that summer that needed medical attention. I could not wiggle my toes or move my ankles. My toes felt like someone had glued them all together. Otherwise, my body seemed to be healing little by little. I was back to sleeping in the waterbed. I could finally wear my jewelry again without it bothering my skin. My skin reaction had settled down and I could see new skin developing and the start of the healing process. I still put lotion all over my skin. I only had a few sores on my feet and the numbness in my arms and feet had diminished somewhat. My legs still needed a lot of work and my right hand was in a claw-like position. I still had a slight limp with my left leg and I was having a lot of headaches that would not go away. I was still kind of drowsy in the morning and still had to take pain medicine at night.

I had dropped the Prednisone completely by November of 1996. At about the same time, I started to feel depressed and could not imagine why. I had an "I don't care" attitude. To cheer myself up, Ally and I took a trip to visit my mother. The visit didn't help cheer me up, however. I started to get the sniffles and felt run down. The day after we arrived, I had a full-fledged cold and a mild temperature. I was blowing my nose all weekend and felt very weak. Rick called the next day and said they were having a snowstorm. He didn't want me to drive home the next day and said to stay another day. I wondered if I could get rid of the cold in the meantime. By that evening I had the chills. The next morning I felt weak and tired. I managed the six-hour drive, and went to bed as soon as we got home.

The next few days I stayed in bed but I couldn't get rid of the cold. Depression had also set in. The depression got worse day by day. It was so intense that nothing mattered to me. I couldn't seem to do anything. I felt so desolate and because I couldn't even cook or clean, it made me feel even worse. I could barely get out of bed to take my daughter to school. I couldn't even watch TV, because I could not concentrate on it. Every day I looked forward to going to bed so I could sleep through my depression. The depression was the most horrible feeling I have ever experienced and one that I would never want to wish on anyone.

I knew there was something wrong with me. It was beginning to be too much. We decided to make an appointment with my doctor in Madison. He had me come up the same day. My doctor thought I had pneumonia again and put me back in the hospital. They performed a procedure on me that involved putting a tube in my nose, down my throat, and into my stomach.

It was very scary when they discussed the procedure with me. But, before they did the procedure they gave me Valium. With that drug, they could have cut my leg off and I wouldn't have cared. The procedure was used to determine what kind of pneumonia I had. I also discussed my major depression. I had just quit taking the Prednisone completely, and it was thought the depression could possibly be from that. (I wished I had known that before.) They put me on Prozac and I hoped that it would work quickly.

They also had to put an IV in me again to give me the antibiotic for the pneumonia. I dreaded it. It took them three hours to get it in. I lost count of how many nurses had tried. They even called the paramedic from the helicopter to try. He failed. Then, a doctor who suddenly appeared in my room took the IV and inserted it in my hand the first time. As he was walking out the door, he looked back and said, "That is why I get paid the big bucks." I love that man.

They were finally able to connect me to the antibiotic IV. Then a lab technician came in and wanted to get some blood from me. I told her, "Over my dead body." No one was going to poke at me anymore that day. I had enough. My nurse agreed.

It was when the IV had been successfully inserted and connected that I had been wheeled down to surgery for the throat procedure. Both the nurse and technician had gotten lost and could not find where we were supposed to go. I was in and out of elevators for about one-half hour. It wouldn't have been so bad, but I was depressed and felt awful due to the pneumonia. My hand hurt from all the pokes, and I had one of those stupid gowns on and was laying on the bed with no covers, being wheeled all over the hospital. I wanted to punch someone.

Within two days, the Prozac had started to work its miracles. I was getting out of my depression. I talked to another leukemia patient and she told me she had the same thing. She had only taken the Prozac a couple of months to level off and then didn't need it anymore. It was like postpartum depression. The only thing I had to deal with was diarrhea from the antibiotics. I went home on the fifth day after I arrived.

A week before Christmas we headed out for the annual Christmas celebration on Rick's side of the family. It was now a small but nice gathering since most of the kids were grown. The following week, we traveled to my side of the family. My brother had all the relatives over to his huge house and we had a wonderful time. It had been a long time since Rick and Brian had been there and everyone was glad to see them. We had a wonderful family Christmas.

The first week of February 1997, my pneumonia came back. This time I went to the emergency room in town. They admitted me right away. They had just opened up the new oncology wing and everything was brand new. It was a very cheerful and spacious room. I was not feeling too bad and they said I would be able to go home in a day or two. There was a lady right across the hall from me. We met in the hallway and started a conversation. She had just been diagnosed with leukemia and was getting ready for a bone marrow transplant. I felt deja vu. I sat her down and told her all about it. She informed me that her husband also needed someone to talk to. I called Rick and told him about the situation. He came to the hospital right away and talked to the husband for quite awhile. I thought it was very good therapy for him. He had not really talked to anyone about it before.

I was discharged the next day. I decided that from that moment on, hospital stays would be a thing of the past for me. I was now going to make my own reality. It was time to get strong, help others and get on with life. I had a destiny.

The lady I had talked to in the hospital about the bone marrow transplant called and told me everything was ready for her to go into the hospital for the transplant the upcoming Monday, but her sister, the donor, had a heart attack that weekend. How bizarre that was I thought. Thank goodness another sibling matched and she would only have to wait a few more weeks to get ready for the transplant. I wished her luck and told her I would keep in touch.

I decided to call two other leukemia patients I had met to see how they were doing. They had some problems that we discussed but said everything else seemed to go okay. I also called Helga, the German lady I had first met in the hospital. She was back in the hospital. Her leukemia had come back. I went to see her and asked if she had any siblings. She only had a brother who lived in Germany. The last time he came to visit, he said he did not want to be a donor. I asked her for his address. I went home and started to write a letter to him. I begged him to at least get tested to see if he was a match and informed him of the seriousness of his sister's disease. I sent the letter to Germany with a self-addressed, stamped envelope.

My brother telephoned and informed me that one of his friends had just been diagnosed with leukemia. I knew what I had to do. As soon as I had hung up, I called him. He was already in a Minnesota hospital. We talked quite awhile and I gave him some insight and encouragement. His spirit was up and he sounded positive. I then wished him good luck. A few days later, my brother called to let me know that he had gone into cardiac arrest that afternoon. I was shocked and immediately called the hospital to talk to his wife. I felt so bad. He died that night. I felt so much compassion for the family.

In May, my husband wanted me to try and work in the office for a couple of hours a day to get me out of the house. I reluctantly went. The first day I came home exhausted. I just crawled into bed. My feet were in constant pain. My skin was still stiff and hard and I ached all over. My right wrist would not move and my fingers were in a claw position. Both my ankles felt very tight. Three days later, I had developed a cough. I started to get the chills that night and by morning I had a temperature of 100 degrees. I had some antibiotics on hand the doctor had given me for just this sort of occasion. I started to take them and stayed in bed for three days. As I was lying in bed, I visualized little laser beams killing the bad cells in my body. I chased them all over inside my body from head to toe, shooting them with a beam of light. I desperately didn't want to go back to the hospital again. I finally had victory. My immune system fought it off without a hospital stay.

My physical therapist called and said he had met a lady who had just been diagnosed with leukemia and asked if I would talk to her. Without any hesitation, I dialed her number. We talked a long time and decided to go to lunch the next day.

We hit it off right away. I gave her a lot of insight into what Leukemia is all about. She also would be having a transplant in Madison with her sibling as a donor. I offered to take her up there on her next appointment to show her around. I called the other two ladies I had talked to previously about their transplants to discuss their progress. Both were doing well and getting on with their lives. I was glad they were doing fine. Helping others gives me a strength inside that I can't describe.

Four years had passed since my transplant when I received a letter from Helga's brother. I immediately called Helga, and her husband informed me she was in the hospital again. Since the letter was in German, I drove to the hospital to have Helga translate. A German doctor had concluded that her brother was too old and weak to do the transplant. Even though there was disappointment in Helga's eyes, I could also see that her brother's letter really meant something to her. I told her when she was able to leave the hospital and got stronger, I would take her to see my doctor in Madison. She agreed. She also confided in me that she had always wanted to go to the casino boats just one time. I told her I should be able to arrange that with no problem.

I felt better as time passed and was reading many books about New Age. There was a whole new section in the library full of books on the subject. Our support group even went to a lecture by Bernie Siegel. The theory of mind, body connection had finally stirred the medical community.

A friend of mine introduced me to an organization in town that offered programs to stimulate awareness, spiritual growth, psychological well being, and creative development. She suggested it would get me on the right path. The two women who run the center provided an environment of support that offered honesty, compassion, challenge and spiritual growth. I decided to take some classes. It turned out to be one of the best decisions I made. It was a home away from home for me.

A few weeks later Helga called and invited me to go to the boats. I gladly said yes and that I would be a friend. I knew Helga and the support group leader, Angie, were close so I decided to call Angie to be the friend I would bring, as a surprise to Helga. Without hesitation, she accepted the invitation. I knew Helga would be glad I chose Angie. As we entered the bus, Helga's eyes were filled with tears and she gave me a big hug. She was overjoyed to see her support group leader friend. I was blessed with happiness. As Angie and I were sitting together, I asked her if she could tell me about the red-haired girl I saw in support group awhile ago, and that I would like to know her name. Angie informed me the girl's name was Carrie, a wonderful human being with a big heart who came from a wonderful family. Angie also knew Carrie's mother. I finally had a name for the face I knew so well. I felt a sense of peace. We all had a great time and Helga enjoyed herself immensely.

My 12-year-old daughter and myself took a clay class together. She had felt down since starting junior high at our local public school and I wanted us to do something together. We had to pick something we wanted to make and she decided on a clay elephant. As we were finishing the project, the teacher came over and asked what the deep blue lines were under the elephant eyes. My daughter immediately blurted out they were tears because the elephant was very sad.

I knew Ally had been down and out about school, but had been blind to how bad it really was for her. Her attitude had been a somber one. The smiling, happy go lucky child I once knew in grade school was nowhere to be found. She frequently went to bed with a stomachache and would wake up to immense stomach pains. I took her to the doctor to find out if there was a problem but he could not find anything wrong with her. She wanted so desperately to be home schooled. She hated school and just wanted to get out. My husband and I pondered on the situation. We asked ourselves, "Is school that bad? Should we make her tough it out?"

I talked to other mothers and students and they said the first year at junior high was rough and that it was a hard adjustment to make from grade school. We wondered whether we should have her change schools. My daughter insisted she did not want to change schools. She just wanted to be home schooled. I wondered if I could handle such an enormous task. "What could be so bad that she wants out of school," I asked myself.

I discussed the problem with her teachers and they said they were not aware of or had not seen anything they felt was going wrong for Ally. Her teachers said she was the ideal student and to their knowledge she was not having any problems. I sat her down and tried to discuss the problem with her. She could not tell me much except that she hated it so. I could not get any answers from her. She began to withdraw.

Then, one night I had a dream. I dreamt I was overlooking an indoor swimming pool. There was an elephant wading backwards, coming towards me. As it came near it bumped into my bed, which was at the end of the swimming pool. In the dream, I looked and saw that my husband was fast asleep. The elephant then transformed into a white horse and reared up onto the bed. I knew it was not there to hurt us, but to get our attention somehow. Then all of a sudden a skylight opened up on the roof and it started to pour rain. The white horse then jumped into the pool and changed again into a whale-like mammal. It jumped up and wailed in the pouring rain.

This dream stayed with me for days and would not go away. I could not understand it. Then it occurred to me. The elephant clay project, the tears of the elephant, the sadness of her hating school. Why did I not see the obvious? I seriously discussed the dream with my husband and realized what we had to do. When Ally came home from school, I discussed with her the decision Rick and I had made. I would home school her the rest of junior high. For the first time in a long time I saw a flicker of hope in her eyes. A slight smile crossed her lips and tension left her face. "How soon?" she asked. "As soon as the home school books arrive in the mail and all the paperwork is done," I told her. (I had called Rick's sister-in-law who had been home schooling her children and had asked her about where to start. She gave me all the information I needed.)

"One more week of school and you will be done," I told Ally. When that week was over, we went to a friend's house for a birthday party. The grandmother of the birthday girl set me aside and asked what I had done. She had never seen my daughter so full of life and so happy. With a smile on my face I replied, "Her dream just came true!"

Chapter 14

Five-Year Survival

*The answer to life can only be found
from within oneself*

On March 3, 1998, I was in my computer room minding my own business. I had decided to work on my book again. When I opened the lower right drawer of my desk, an overwhelming emotional thought came to the front of my mind. It was very clear and without a shadow of doubt. My angel had appeared to me. She revealed herself shyly to me. It was Carrie. I immediately felt humbly embarrassed. For a long time I had felt guilty about not helping her, while at the same time she was *helping* me.

How could I have not seen it before? I must have been blind. This vision or thought stayed with me for days. I desperately wanted to tell someone, but I knew there was no one to tell. I feared I would be ridiculed. But I knew I would never deny that I felt her with me. She had been at my side all the time. Her energy filled my heart. (No, I was not on any drugs.)

My mother and father-in-law owned a summer home in Florida and had been asking us for the past couple of years to come down and visit. I decided to take them up on it. After everything Ally had been through with me, I wanted to make it up to her and have some fun.

Rick decided to stay behind and let Ally and I have some time together. We left O'Hare and arrived at Orlando Airport, where Rick's parents picked us up. We drove a little over an hour to their summer condo. The condo was a luxurious two-bedroom decorated in exquisite taste. A swimming pool and Jacuzzi were at the center of the condos. From this day forward, Ally and I were spoiled immensely and were not allowed to pay for anything. We were chauffeured to Disneyland, Universal Studios, and Cypress Gardens. Since I could not walk very well or long, they insisted I get a wheelchair. I was wheeled everywhere I went. I was quite embarrassed by it, but I also knew I would hold everyone up without the use of a wheelchair. The experience was something I will never forget. Before we left, I thanked them for a wonderful vacation. It had definitely brought my daughter and myself closer together.

Five years had passed since my transplant. In the previous year, I had only needed to take one prescription drug once a day to prevent infection and an occasional pain pill. My ankles were still stiff and sore, I still walked with a limp on my left knee and my right hand was still in a claw-like position with hardly any movement to the wrist. I still had some lesions on my foot. My blood counts had all been normal for years and I never needed a blood transfusion. I had the secure feeling that the leukemia was not going to come back.

About a month after our vacation to Florida, I took Helga to my doctor in Madison. I also had an appointment with him to discuss going to John Hopkins for my GVHD. He gave me his approval. Helga and I stopped for coffee on the way back. Over coffee, she told me that my doctor was a very nice man, but he had to tell her the truth about her condition. He had told her that her age and condition would not allow her to handle a bone marrow transplant and there was nothing he could do for her. I think she already knew but needed someone to actually say it to her. She was graciously thankful. We talked about her family and how she was preparing for her death.

The next day, I phoned John Hopkins University in Baltimore, Maryland to set up an appointment. I had first learned of the John Hopkins GVHD consultation clinic on the Internet. They had a team of experts who were trying various ongoing approaches of therapy to help GVHD patients. The oncology center had faxed me the necessary papers my doctor and I needed to fill out and fax back. Appointments are always made for two days, on a Thursday and Friday. I discussed my problem with them. They informed me that they could help and had a lot of protocols. I told them about my experience with certain drugs I could not take and they took that into consideration. With the blessing of my bone marrow transplant doctor, I went ahead and scheduled a visit with John Hopkins Hospital.

My sister chose to come along to keep me company. She flew into Chicago O'Hare, where we met and boarded a plane to Baltimore. We arrived at the airport and got a cab to take us to Hope Lodge. Hope Lodge is conveniently located near the University of Maryland Cancer Center and is within a ten-minute ride to John Hopkins Oncology Center. When I called to make my appointment, I was put on a waiting list to stay at the lodge.

If an opening came about I wouldn't need to pay for a hotel, since John Hopkins had made lodging arrangements. We settled in and explored the lodge. The lodge provided a home-like surrounding including guest bedrooms with private baths, a central kitchen, dining room, library and an enclosed garden. It was very neat and clean. The place was so quiet that it felt deserted. The Ronald McDonald House for Children was across the street. I wished I could visit the children there. After a long day we retired and got ready for the two-day appointments starting early the following morning.

We arrived at the hospital, with the lodge providing transportation, early in the morning for the first appointment. I would be evaluated by a multidisciplinary team of marrow transplant personnel, dermatologists, ophthalmologists, physician assistants, nurses, social workers, therapists and several other experts who would discuss a protocol to fit my needs.

I spent most of the morning and early afternoon being analyzed by several experts. I had the rest of the day off, and the nurse suggested some tourist attractions we could see. I only had one more appointment the next morning to see the physical therapist at a different facility across town. My sister Joanne and I decided to take the nurse's advice and explore Baltimore. We grabbed a cab and headed down to The Inner Harbor. The Inner Harbor is like a mall with shops all around the Bay. In the middle of the Bay is the National Aquarium. Since we had plenty of time, we decided to explore the aquarium and had an enjoyable day. One particular restaurant was noted for their crab cakes and we decided to have supper there.

After getting back to the lodge, we telephoned an old neighbor from our hometown, Donna, and decided to meet with her for brunch Saturday morning. Donna extended an offer to take us to the airport for our upcoming flight home.

Friday morning, we arrived at the physical therapy building. The doctor did a complete physical on me and wanted me to see both physical and occupational therapists when I arrived home. All of the experts who had analyzed me were going to prepare reports and a protocol would be sent to my oncology doctor to be approved.

My appointments at John Hopkins were completed. Joanne and I grabbed a cab and talked about what to do. Since Washington D.C. was close by, we decided to take the train into Union Station and explore Washington D.C. By the time we arrived, it was dark. We walked out of Union Station for a short distance to The White House and took some pictures. Then, we caught a bus and headed to Georgetown, where there are many shops and restaurants. After about an hour, we took a cab back to Union Station and waited for the next train to Penn Station in Baltimore. I was exhausted but glad we toured Washington. I tried not to let my disability get in the way of anything I wanted to do. Mind over matter.

As soon as we arrived at the lodge, I fell asleep. The next morning Donna picked us up at the lodge and we had wonderful conversation at brunch. We thanked her for the ride to the airport and arrived home safe and sound by nightfall.

Three weeks later, my doctor received the report from John Hopkins. They wanted to put me in a clinical trial using several different powerful drugs that had many side effects. We both agreed not to put me on the FK-506 drug due to the complications I had with Cyclosporine in the past. I also expressed my concern over using the menopausal drugs they had suggested.

We decided to just stay with the Premarin cream, a high dose calcium supplement, and measure my bone density periodically. My main concern was to get my skin back to normal. They offered some other alternatives with less toxic side effects. We decided to start the drug called Cellcept (the generic name is Mycophenolate Mofetilat) at a very low dose and return to physical and occupational therapy. Since using this drug could bring about an increased chance of infection, I would also take TMP/sulfa twice daily on weekends. I wished there were a natural way or some other alternative than taking more drugs.

When I started taking the Cellcept, 500mg twice a day, I started to experience severe headaches, stomachaches and dizziness. We decided to drop the drug dosage down to one pill a day. My body seemed to tolerate this better. On Monday I decided to try physical and occupational therapy at another facility where I would receive more individual attention. I started to go three times a week.

On my first visit, the therapist tried to stretch my feet and the skin ripped. I knew the therapist felt bad, but it actually did some good. It was painful, but when it grew back it, there was more skin. We did physical and occupational therapy for about three months with little improvement. The effects of stretching did not last long. When the skin was pulled, it would stretch, but after letting go, it would bounce back to its original position. It was very frustrating and I decided to give it up. The drug Cellcept was not making any improvements to my skin either, and my doctor and I agreed to discontinue it.

I had been thinking about Carrie and her family for quite some time. I wanted so desperately to meet them. How could I tell them what had happened to me and not have them think I should be committed? I took a drive a week before the holidays in the vicinity of the street they lived on. As I got to the intersection and turned onto their street, I knew instantly which house they lived in without looking at the address. I felt immense energy and just knew. It didn't look like anyone was home. I wanted so much to knock on the door and hug her family and talk to them, but it would all sound too crazy. I had also been looking at angels that helped people with breast cancer to see if any of them were named Carrie, but there were none. I wanted something to give her mother when I finally got up enough courage to see her.

I don't know what it is about me, but I had to get out of the area every so often or I felt like I would go crazy. I love to travel. I always seemed to have energy when I traveled. Rick suggested I should try to look up my relatives in Italy and plan a trip with my sister. I thought it would be a good idea. We had recently come upon some extra money and I decided to pay my sister's way. I had always wanted to do something for her for giving me my life back. I first wrote to the town where my grandparents came from to see if there were any relatives still alive there. I knew my grandfather's generation had owned an Italian bakery. They brought that tradition to America and established a bakery where my father had once worked. I received a letter back and an address of a relative. To my surprise, the bakery still existed. I sent a letter to the bakery and in a matter of weeks received a letter back expressing great excitement. They insisted we stay with them to meet all our relatives, which were many.

The first week, my sister and I would take a tour of Italy and the second week we would take time to be with our relatives. My brother decided to join us. Everything was set and everyone in the family knew about it except my sister. I had telephoned her place of work to make sure she could take two weeks off in July of the following year. I decided to surprise her at Christmas and could not wait to see the expression on her face.

For a couple of months, I spent time on numerous visits to the dentists. I had healthy teeth before the transplant, but after the transplant every tooth in my mouth needed to be pulled or worked on. Going to the dentist was one more thing I had to withstand.

Rick called me from the office and asked me if I wanted to go to Maui. At first, I wasn't sure what a Maui was and asked him to repeat it. It just so happened that the couples we had gone with to Jamaica were planning a vacation and wanted us to join them. Without hesitation, I accepted the invitation.

We would all be getting a condo and share the expenses. I reminded him of the Italy trip and was concerned whether we could afford this. He reassured me we could manage it. As I hung up the phone, I began to realize how far we had come since I was first diagnosed with leukemia. We had to downsize our life for a couple of years. We sold one of our vehicles and had to refinance our home just to pay for the medical bills. We ate many boxes of macaroni and cheese those years.

A few days before Christmas, I made a poster board with all the towns we would be touring in Italy. I rolled it up and wrapped it in Christmas paper. I put it in a big box and wrapped the box. We were leaving to visit my mother the next day and celebrate Christmas. Everyone was excited about seeing Joanne's expression when she opened her present. I was so glad I could give her this wonderful gift.

On Christmas Eve I gave the last present under the tree to my wonderful sister. We were all filled with excitement as she unraveled the mystery. She was in total shock and could hardly talk. We both gave each other a hug and I told her how thankful I was and how much I appreciated her for giving me my life back. The weekend was spent discussing our trip.

Reading books in bed had become one of my favorite pastimes. Taking classes at our local college and at my woman's organization on various different subjects had also been one of my passions. Some of these classes included Ayurveda, meditation and the chakras. I hungered for knowledge. One particular, interesting class was on coincidences.

Chapter 15

Healing the Mind, Body, and Soul

Life is like a canvas
Paint your own picture.

My mother arrived at our house the weekend before we planned to go to Maui. She would stay with Ally. I was halfway through reading one of James Redfield's books and decided to take it with me.

After a very long flight, we arrived in Maui, Hawaii. I had always wanted to visit Maui and never dreamed I would be here so soon. We picked up our rental car and drove to our condo. We had a lovely view of the ocean on our terrace. We unpacked, found a grocery store and loaded up the condo with food. One of the girls wanted to read what I had written so far of my book. I had brought the rough draft in a scenic folder that Ally had bought for school. I handed her the folder and hoped she would be an honest critic.

We decided to explore downtown. One couple wanted to go into the art galleries to look for paintings. I leisurely walked in with them, disinterested. We finally left and went back to the condo.

The next day, we drove the long route to what is known as *The Road to Hana,* a very winding road that grips the mountainside. It is a beautiful, magical place of incredible waterfalls surrounded by lush tropical forests. We stopped just above the Black Sand Beach to view the scenery. The waves violently crashed onto the cliffs with enormous force. An opening in one of the rocks would shoot water out like a torpedo, crashing down on anything in its path. The scenery mesmerized us. It was an awesome sight. At every turn in the road we made, gorgeous waterfalls would appear. It was a wonderful experience.

The next day we walked around downtown in and out of art galleries. Inside one, a painting caught my eye. It looked familiar. I walked outside to read the sign that indicated who the painter was. I walked back in and asked my friend to take a look at the painter's name. She thought it was the same name in the scenic folder that my rough draft was in. When we got back to the condo, we confirmed it was the same painting and same author on the folder as the one in the gallery. I grabbed the book I had been reading by James Redfield and it too had a similar painting on the jacket cover. It was of course a painting of, what else but a beautiful waterfall in a secret place. Talk about coincidences. But exactly what did it all mean? What connection or sign was it telling me?

We did an abundant amount of sightseeing and spent some time on the beach. According to my doctor, if I wore sunscreen, it would be good for my skin to be exposed to some sun, since it had been deprived of it for several years.

A few weeks after we returned home from Maui, I felt determined to find a solution for the condition of my skin and claw-like hands. I searched the Internet, and talked to other patients who were also suffering from GVHD. One particular study used light treatments to even out the skin. I pulled up all the information I could on this subject. I learned that there were two kinds of light therapy. One is called PUVA and the other is UVB. Both PUVA and UVB treatments are used primarily for psoriasis patients, but some studies showed slight improvement with GVHD of the skin. Since every medical profession needs a referral, I called my doctor to write up an order.

PUVA treatments usually take place in a dermatologist's office. A Psoralen pill is taken 75 to 90 minutes before entering the UVA light box. The treatment itself is like going to a tanning bed. You stand up in a box with UVA bulbs surrounding you. Goggles must be worn at all times in the booth. Special sunglasses must be used when the sun is shining, for 24 hours before and after treatment. Exposure time is gradually increased over time. On average, 25 treatments are administered. I decided to try this out before my trip to Italy in July. I noticed a great improvement in my skin color. The lesions begin to dry up. When I returned from Italy, we would switch to the UVB treatment. The difference between the two is that UVB does not require taking a pill or wearing the sunglasses before and after treatment because it is not as intense as UVA.

Joanne arrived from Duluth at O'Hare airport where I met her for the long flight to Italy. We could not believe we were actually going. My brother had no interest in touring Italy the first week, so we planned to meet him in Venice at the end of our tour. The tour was more than we could have hoped for. It was an experience we will never forget.

Our relatives picked us up at our hotel in Venice, where we had met our brother. All of us were a little anxious and nervous at our first meeting with our relatives at the hotel. We all then left the hotel and arrived about one hour later at a place high in the mountains, where our grandparents once had lived so long ago. Thank goodness we had a translator with us most of the time so we could communicate. We all had a wonderful time meeting such nice people. We enjoyed our new big family and shared our different cultures.

A few days after returning home and recuperating from the trip to Italy, I telephoned Helga to see how she was doing. She had been in bed feeling sick and very tired. I wished her well and told her I hoped that we would get together when she was feeling better. I called the other girls to see how they were doing. Everyone was fine and one of them was also trying the PUVA lighting for their skin. We compared notes.

One day, I was passing a shop near my house and looked up. I stopped dead in my tracks. There in the window were beautiful angels, done in cross-stitch. I stepped into the shop and inquired about how much they were. Unfortunately, they were not for sale. I knew that was what I had to get for Carrie's mother. The shopkeeper showed me where all the angel booklets were and I started to thumb through them. I gasped when I found an angel standing by a small tree. She had red hair. I knew instantly that would be the one. I decided to sign up for classes. When I took the class, I realized my hands could not make the stitch. I would have to find someone else to do it for me somehow.

Karen, my friend, came over to visit the very next day. I told her about the angel. She immediately called her sister, who said she would be glad to do it. I felt so graciously honored by her thoughtfulness. Excitedly, I telephoned Angie and told her how I wanted to make Carrie's mother this angel, and described the project to her. I also mentioned to her how close I felt towards her, without mentioning my vision. She was so moved by it that she too got excited and said the mother would just adore it. I wanted it to be done by Christmas but since it was almost Thanksgiving, it would be difficult to accomplish. I asked when Carrie had died. Angie told me it had been sometime in June. So, I decided to give it to her on that same day.

I asked Angie if she knew what color eyes Carrie had, to make sure we got it right on the angel. Since I had only met her once and really didn't get a real good look at her, I wasn't sure. Angie was not sure but knew she had a picture of Carrie somewhere and would give me a call back and let me know. I was appreciative. I hung up the phone and felt a kind of energy again. I put my swimsuit on, went out into the Jacuzzi, put some soothing music on and stared at the sky. I felt so at peace and serene. I thanked Carrie for being in my life. I don't know if it was my imagination or what, but she suddenly appeared to me in my mind and we were both in the meadow again. She was smiling and took my hand. In a second, we were on top of a mountain and she wanted me to look down. I did, but could not see anything. I sensed that it was where she lived. She looked serene and at peace, but I could not see what was there. She smiled and took me back to the meadow and waved goodbye, and off she went up the mountain.

A few days later I received a letter from Angie. I knew the picture of Carrie would be in it. I was afraid to open it up. When I did, I did not recognize the person in the picture. At first I felt this was the wrong person. Then I remembered that I did not really get a good look at her face years ago. I had only felt her emotions. Then something came over me and told me to look at the picture with my heart and not my eyes. I closed my eyes and felt her energy. It was Carrie. She had just taught me a valuable lesson.

Helga's husband called and informed me that Helga had had a major stroke and was in the hospital in a coma. She didn't have much time left. I went that night to say goodbye to Helga. I stayed for awhile and held her cold hand. I talked to her family. Somehow I was not afraid of death anymore. I looked at her lying there holding on with each breath. I wanted to tell her it was okay to go. She had suffered enough and needed to be at peace. She had told me the last time she was in the hospital that she was ready to go. She had accepted the ultimate fate. I only hoped that she had not suffered those 48 hours she was in a coma and had left us in peace and tranquillity. There would be no more pain. She truly was finally at rest.

I wanted to have surgery on my hand to get it straightened out. I decided to go to the orthopedic doctor in Madison. The doctor would not do surgery. He wanted me to try therapy again. I was very disappointed.

He told me that a hand therapist who used to work with him now worked in Rockford and he wanted me to go see her. What a coincidence that was. So they had me set up an appointment with her for the following week, the week before Thanksgiving. The therapist decided to cast my fingers for a week to see if the skin would stretch. After a week, it looked like they had stretched a little. We decided to cast the right wrist to try and get some movement out of it. Amazingly, when we took the cast off the wrist moved back and forth. There were wrinkles at the wrist, which made the skin flexible so that it would move.

Next, we decided to make a cast that could be taken off and also added pulleys to each finger so they would pull down the fingers to stretch them. Each finger would have a small cuff to fit into with a string attached to it. Then a piece of Velcro would be attached to the string so I could pull it down and stretch the finger to the opposite Velcro. This seemed to help. Next time we met, we took the mobile cast off and did ultrasound on each finger. Slowly, we saw improvement. My skin was finally healed enough to stretch and was permanently staying stable. I also started physical therapy on my ankles. They too started to move. I was determined to be a normal human being with all normal functions. This looked like the beginning of the end.

During the Thanksgiving weekend, I went to a class on hydrotherapy. When I got home from class, I made a visualization tape for myself to listen to everyday to help heal myself. I was determined to have my hand healed this time using therapy and alternative medicine.

*   *   *

It is now the beginning of a new millennium I look back at my life and all that I have experienced. I have to stop and wonder about all of it. I know I would never wish this upon anyone else. I have learned so much each step of the way and believe that all of the experiences I have had happened to me for a good reason. I still think about the comedian that was in my mind. He always made me laugh when I was down. I can't help but smile every time I see a picture of him. Did it really happen? Did the drugs just enhance it? Only God knows. I will also remember the vision of my father and the emotion that I felt at that time. And my angel, as God is my witness, is real to me. We have come too far together and I don't care what anyone thinks anymore. It is my reality or dream as some may want to call it.

I still can't help but think of those people that were in the psychiatric ward. I wonder what happened to them. Did they ever get normal and solve their demons from within? I still believe so much in faith and God. My life has been so turned around from all that has happened to me so far. I know for the better. I now help when I see a handicapped person in need. I visit and call people who have leukemia. I try to comfort them and help them get through the bad times. I would like to help others feel strong and give them hope and strength. It gives me so much pleasure and strength in return.

I have also met Carrie's mother and father, two wonderful people. Carrie's mother has stated that meeting me has given her much joy, because Carrie's last words were, "Mom, will anyone remember me?" I have decided to place the finished, framed, angel of Carrie in the Angel Museum in Beloit, Wisconsin, where Oprah Winfrey has donated some of her angels for everyone to see.

I feel so great and loving of this whole world that God has made for us. I finally found peace and love and know in what direction I need to go. It does not matter what religion you practice, because in the long run, we are all ONE. We are now living and growing in a more spiritual world than ever before. Believe in yourself. Learn to forgive and love yourself and help others. If you have that, then you can conquer anything in this world. Words cannot express how lovingly I feel towards my sister for giving me a second chance on life. Thank you from the bottom of my heart. I notice the sun is brighter, the clouds whiter, and the sky is a vibrant blue. And if I look real hard, everything around me is illuminating. I think I finally found out what life is all about and now I want to

"S O A R" !!!

A Donor's Message

My name is Joanne and I am Frances's older sister. We were very close growing up and we became even closer when I became a very important part of my sister's life, even more important than I could have ever imagined. I would like to tell you about my feelings and experiences that began in 1991, late in December.

Your world can change in a moment's time. You realize when the change occurs, just how precious time is. My sister was diagnosed with leukemia in December, 1991. I still remember the call. The exact words are a blur, but the shocking word "leukemia" rang loud in my ears. When you get news like this, your mind freezes, your heart skips a beat and then it beats faster and harder. You hope you misunderstood, because you don't want to believe the news. You think, "Maybe this is all a dream?" A feeling of heaviness fills within you and your mind is darting in so many directions that you feel completely helpless at first. Could the doctor have made a mistake? Was it really true? After analyzing the facts, I had to accept reality. My sister had leukemia.

I gave myself time to realize what this really meant and then asked myself what I could do to help. I knew the first thing I had to do was to give support and encouragement to her and her family and to mine and then be positive, no matter how hopeless the situation seemed to be. Being positive was exactly what my sister needed to be, and that she was. She thought positively, which made me feel better because I knew she would fight this as much as she could. She had an unbelievable driving determination to beat this disease.

In the days and months that followed for the first year, I was filled with many ups and downs. My sister had many obstacles to overcome and I was always so proud of her for that. All of the tests and treatments, the office visits, the hospital stays, and change of doctors always weighed heavily on my heart.

After each doctor appointment, I would wait for her call to come. Each time the phone rang on the day of an appointment, I would jump and my heart would beat fast. It's hard to explain how emotional waiting for news can be. Her calls would come and I could hear it in her voice if her tests were good and her treatments were keeping her leukemia away. She would say, "I'm still clear of leukemia," and then my spirit would lift and I would be so happy for her.

Early into her treatments, a bone marrow transplant was mentioned, and my brother and I were given blood tests to determine if either of us were a match for our sister. I prayed that one of us would be a match so that we could help our younger sister through this. When I found out that I was a perfect match, I was so thankful that I would be able to give her my bone marrow for a transplant. I didn't feel so helpless anymore and I knew that together we could make this work. You can't believe the feeling you have inside when you know that you will be able to allow someone else to continue to live. It is something you can't explain, but I felt so fortunate to be able to give her that chance.

Then her call came after one of her doctor's appointments, a year and a half after she was diagnosed with leukemia, and she said to me, "What are your doing on July 29?" I knew at that moment that her leukemia had come back and she would now have to go through the bone marrow transplant. I knew this was something she had hoped she would not have to go through.

To prepare for the transplant, I was told that I would have to take iron pills for two months prior to the transplant and that a pint of my own blood would be drawn from me and sent to the hospital to be given back to me after the transplant. Then, a day before the transplant, I would have to have a physical examination.

I arrived a day early with my mother and brother, prior to the transplant. I had a physical examination done and then visited with my sister. During the examination I was told not to blame myself if something went wrong after the transplant. But, deep down, I felt peacefulness in my heart and I knew that everything was going to be okay. My sister would have to prepare so much more to receive my bone marrow and to endure the critical days and months that would lie ahead for her.

On the day of the transplant I was admitted early that morning and was prepared for surgery. I chose to remain awake during the procedure, which would take about an hour. I was given a spinal and the doctors extracted what bone marrow they needed from each hip. After the bone marrow was extracted it was harvested and hours later given to my sister through a transfusion. Our families and friends were all with her when she was given my bone marrow and we celebrated with so many different emotions the start of a new beginning for her. I stayed in the hospital that night and I was discharged the next day. The only discomfort I had was that I was a little sore or stiff, but that soon passed. My mother and I stayed the rest of the week to be with her and keep her company and give her support. The following week I went back to work and continued to be on iron pills for two months after the transplant in order to rebuild my bone marrow.

My sister and I have a bond that goes beyond any I could have ever dreamed of. My bone marrow will live inside of her for the rest of her life. She is the person I admire and look up to and am so proud of. She is a most courageous, positive and inspiring person who has affected so many lives during the fight of her life and I am so very proud of her and her family for their victory.

Epilogue

Seven years ago my aunt found out that she had cancer. She had cancer of the blood called leukemia. She was surprised because the type of leukemia she had wasn't a common disease in adults. Soon she began to get very sick and had to stay in the hospital. She was horrified and scared that she would die because of this disease, so that is when she knew that she had to fight the cancer to get healthy again.

Her fight against leukemia began. She had many weeks of chemotherapy, which made her very sick and weak. She needed many blood transfusions during her chemotherapy treatments. She never complained about being in the hospital.

After many long months of fighting the disease, her tests came back that she was free of leukemia. I admired her for being so brave because every month she has to be retested, and then after the fifteenth month, her leukemia had come back. She then had to go through a bone marrow transplant, which took a lot of courage.

I learned from her that you never give up no matter how bad things look, because if you believe in yourself, you can overcome anything. I also learned that it is good to help others because my aunt now goes to different hospitals to give other leukemia patients hope and courage to get better.

I think that my aunt is a role model because of her courage and how she encourages others to strive for things and never give up hope.

11/10/98 Matt

List of Resources

Leukemia Society of America
600 3rd Avenue2900
New York NY 10016
1-800-955-4572
Publications, Support Groups,
Financial Aid

BMT–Newsletter
Skokie Valley Road
Highland Park IL 60035
888-597-7674 or 847-433-4599
Publications, Patient Links

**National Leukemia Research
Association**
585 Stewart Avenue Suite 536
Garden City NY 11530
516-222-1944
Publications, Limited Financial Aid

**Children's Organ Transplant
Association**
2501 Cota Drive
Bloomington IN 47403
800-366-2682
Fundraising Assistance

Leukemia Research Foundation
820 Davis Street
Evanston, IL 60201
847-424-0600
Publications, Support Groups,
Financial Aid
(For people within 100 miles
of Chicago)

The Transplant Foundation
8002 Discovery Drive Suite 310
Richmond VA 23229
804-285-5115
Financial Aid for
Immunosuppressive Drugs

Granny Barb and Art's Leukemia Link
Website: http://www.acor.org/leukemia/
Links to Information on Leukemia and BMT Transplant Survivors

American Cancer Society
800-227-2345

GVHD Buddy Program
1-410-955-6765-Holly Dawsey
Established to help patients support one another Sponsored by John Hopkins Oncology Ctr.

Cancer Treatment Centers of America
1-800-955-2822

Airline Service
1-800-877-Airline
Pilots that Donate their Time to Transport the Sick

Functional Solutions
1-800-235-7054
Magazine Products for Disabilities

Children's Hope and Dreams
973-361-7366
Email:NCSD@AOL.COM
Penpal Programs for Children

Cancer Information Service Bethesda MD
800-422-6237
Website: http://cancernet.nci.nih.gov
(Information on current cancer treatments and clinical trials.)

Natl. Assoc. of Hospital Houses
800-542-9730 or 301-961-5264
Website: www.nahh.com
Referrals to Free or Low Cost Lodging

Beauty Trends (Revlon wigs)
1-800-777-7772
Free catalog to order inexpensive wigs.

Coping with Cancer
PO Box 682268
Franklin TN 37068-2268
615-790-2400
Magazine for Anyone Touched by Cancer

OTHER THERAPIES THAT CAN ACCOMPANY CONVENTIONAL THERAPY

The list below includes some of many favorable therapies, enhancing a healthy lifestyle. I have tried each one of these and they have all been very beneficial to me in one way or another. You can find the one that is best for you. Do not think it is going against your own religious beliefs, as some people think. Many teachers who teach these classes are Christians. You can find these classes in your area taught at athletic clubs, Colleges, community services, YMCA, YWCA and other various organizations. We must all work together to heal our minds, bodies, and souls.

YOGA
An Indian exercise to heal the mind as well as the body.

TAI CHI
This Chinese slow form of exercise strengthens your balance.
(I am currently taking this class to strengthen my ankles.)

QIGONG THERAPY
An ancient Chinese technique which allows you to relax and ward off diseases.

REIKI HEALING
This healing system is derived from Tibetan masters. Healing sessions include energy from the practitioners that lightly touch specific body parts. It is useful way to balance any of the four bodies (mental, emotional, physical or spiritual).

HYPNOTHERAPY
Hypnotic technique where the patient is always aware but in a semi-state of consciousness. Hypnosis is a very useful therapeutic tool and can be used to remove unhealthy living habits.

VISUALIZATION THERAPY (Meditation)
This therapy is used to help relax and stimulate positive images to promote mental and emotional health. It is very therapeutic.

REFLEXOLOGY
A map of the patient's body is seen on his/her palm or sole of feet. Applying pressure to specific areas of the body helps stimulate the body's healing system.

THERAPEUTIC MASSAGE
The patient's body is massaged usually using lotions to relieve various disorders. Many different techniques are available.

PRAYER
An expression of thoughts, hopes, or needs directed toward a deity, as for survival.

Portrait of my family two years before being diagnosed.

Losing my first head of hair in February, 1992.

Regrowth of my hair-dark and curly. September 1992.

Standing on top of the El Castillo Pyramid.

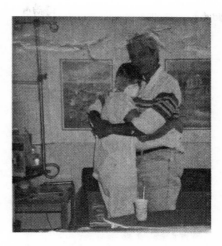

The day of transplant with my husband Rick in July, 1993.

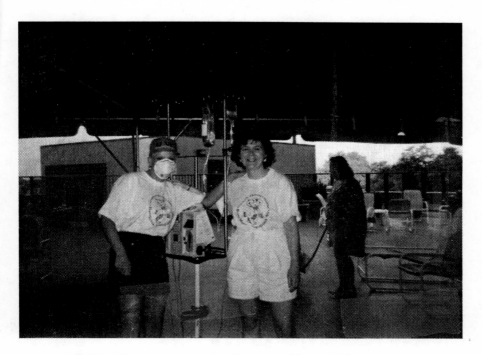

Waiting for the bone marrow to work with my sister, Joanne.

My first day venturing out of the hospital for a few hours of freedom with my daughter, Ally.

One of the many wigs I wore standing with my friend Karen.

Holding my step-grandchild.

Wearing my "Ski Boots" to straighten out my ankles.

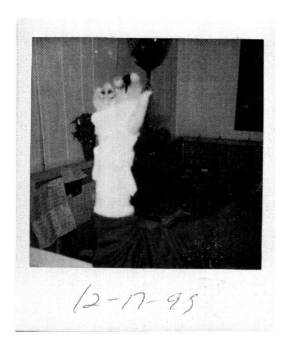

12-17-95

The handmade mobile cast invented by my hand therapist.

Visiting with my favorite nurse, Gail.

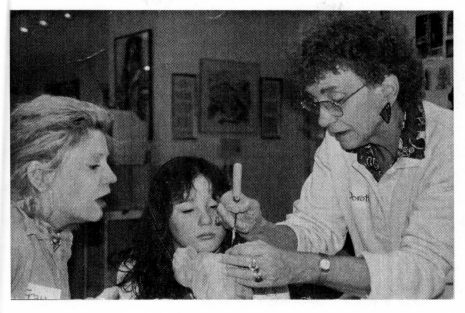

Making our clay elephant with a little help from Dorothy, our instructor.